SECTION

1

BUILDING WEBSITES WITH HTML5 TO WORK WITH MOBILE PHONES

Do you have a mobile phone? Back in the mid-1990s there is a good chance you did not. Today? Well, today, there is a good chance you do not have a landline phone, but you certainly have a mobile phone. According to Gartner, one in three people on the planet have a mobile phone, with that number expected to increase to two in three over the span of this decade. What does that mean? Four billion people will have mobile phones by the year 2020.

Today, mobile phones are broken into three broad categories: call only, feature phone, and smart phone.

The call-only phone allows you to make calls and maybe to send and receive text messages. Nothing fancy. A feature phone comes with a camera, texting, and possibly a Facebook app, as shown in Figure 1.1.

The third category is smart phone. One phone has come to symbolize all smart phones: Apple's iPhone. It is fair to compare the iPhone to a computer. With an iPhone you have the following:

- GPS
- Hi-res camera
- Video recording
- Accelerometer
- Gyroscope
- Internet access

When the iPhone was launched in 2007, Apple CEO Steve Jobs hailed the phone as three devices in one: the best phone, the best iPod, and the best way to experience the web, as shown in Figure 1.2. Using an iPhone to surf the web you will see that the mobile experience is phenomenal. Web pages simply render as they are meant to; *The New York Times* loads correctly, CNN looks like CNN, and Facebook just works.

Figure 1.1 Feature phones.

Figure 1.2 Steve Jobs with the original iPhone presented in January 2007.

The reason for this is due to the browser, Mobile Safari. Mobile Safari is not a stripped-down version of a browser, as you will find in older smart phones such as Windows Mobile 6.5, but a browser that stands shoulder-to-shoulder with leading desktop browsers such as Google's Chrome or Mozilla's Firefox.

Apple is able to do this because Mobile Safari is built on top of the Open Source platform called WebKit. The same WebKit that is used in Mobile Safari is used in the desktop version of Safari and under the hood of Google's Chrome. The key standout feature for WebKit is its massive support for HTML5, the new set of standards that allows you to build print quality websites.

While Apple may have raised the bar for smart phones, it is not the only player in town. It is becoming increasingly clear that Google, with its mobile Android operating system (Figure 1.3), is now standing shoulder-to-shoulder with Apple.

Google's Android OS is now currently the most popular mobile OS for smart phones. There is a simple reason for this: Google gives the OS away for free as an Open Source project. Anyone can download and use the Android OS. They can even customize the OS and control how it is deployed. This is clear when you buy a Verizon phone or an HTC phone. Both run Android, but both can look very different, as shown in Figure 1.4.

At the heart of the Android phone experience is another WebKit-enabled web browser. There are subtle differences between Apple's WebKit implementation and Android's (we will cover that in more detail elsewhere), but on the whole a page that loads in one will load in another.

Today, Android and iPhones are the two leading phones, but the whole smart phone market is very small and is expected to grow exponentially. At the January 2011 quarterly result conference, Tim Cook, Apple's COO, made the comment that "in the future there will not be feature phones or smart phones; they will be all smart phones." Cook's comments are accurate. The rate of adoption of smart phones is like nothing the tech industry has seen. To this end, both Apple and Google are going to find their market space getting very crowded.

During 2011 three strong mobile operating systems will join Android and iOS: Microsoft's Windows Phone 7, RIM's BlackBerry 6, and HP/Palm's WebOS.

Figure 1.3 The Google Android logo.

Figure 1.4 Android running on three different phones from Motorola, HTC, and Samsung.

Figure 1.5 Windows Phone 7 with the unique tile interface.

Microsoft lacked vision when it came to Mobile devices. At one point, Microsoft owned the market. Losing can, sometimes, be a great panacea. Microsoft's response is Windows Phone 7, a solid contender to Apple's iOS (shown in Figure 1.5). The interface is unique, employing a metaphor called tiles. Interestingly, though, when Windows Phone 7 launched, it did not come with an HTML5 browser. Microsoft addressed this issue during the summer of 2011 with a new release of the OS that includes a mobile browser that can view HTML5 websites.

Like, Microsoft, RIM was also a leader of smart phone development. Its response to Apple and Google has been slow, but it is clear that it is coming back with a strong solution in its adoption of the BlackBerry 6 operating system.

HP/Palm's WebOS is, to me, a success story waiting to happen. In many ways, when Palm launched the Pre (shown in Figure 1.6) and Pixi running WebOS, it was the bad hardware, not the OS, that let the product down and eventually saw Palm being purchased by HP. The core development environment for WebOS is HTML5 standards (CSS, HTML, JavaScript, etc.). Powering all this is an implementation of WebKit. HP has already promised that WebOS will be back in style in 2011.

What is becoming clear, in these early days of smart phone development, is that who the leader is today will change every 3 to 6 months. Unlike the days of the web back in the mid-1990s when only two companies were vying for your attention (Netscape and Microsoft), today you have many companies and phone carriers. In addition, buying a new phone every 12 to 18 months for around $100 to $150 is not unreasonable. Indeed,

Figure 1.6 WebOS running on a Palm Pre.

Apple has an agreement with AT&T that allows you to upgrade your phone every 12 months. The smart phone replacement cycle is forcing companies to upgrade their software and hardware on a rapid curve. Think about this for a moment: the smart phone category we think of today did not exist until mid-2007. Only four years ago.

If you look at all five companies, Apple, Google, Microsoft, RIM, and HP, and their mobile operating systems, one single common thread can be seen among all of them: HTML5-enabled browsing.

Designing for the Mobile Web

Designing websites for a smart phone is not the same as designing for a PC web browser. There are several top-level differences you need to consider when designing for mobile devices:

- Screen size
- Changing portrait/landscape views
- High-quality resolution
- Input devices
- HTML5 support

Over the last few years, a widescreen aspect has become the norm for many laptop screen sizes. Typical screen sizes now run 1280×1024 pixels. In contrast, the first iPhone ran at 320×480 pixels. The Android OS can run many different screen resolutions (top-level devices such as the HTC EVO runs at 800×480; whereas the entry level Android phones have a screen resolution of 240×400). The iPhone 4 and 5 both have a screen resolution of 960×640, double the size of the first three generations of iPhone.

Physically, smart phones are unlikely to increase much more in screen resolution for a simple reason: a phone cannot be too large, otherwise you will not be able to hold it with one hand. Dell's Android-powered Streak failed because it was too large to hold with one hand. Come on, people, this is not 1989 anymore (check out Gordon Gekko's phone in *Wall Street*—wow!).

In addition to a smaller screen, web pages on smart phones have a second, unique experience: constant change between landscape and portrait view. All the leading smart phones will allow you to twist your phone around to get a better view of the web page. Hardware accelerators in the phone can detect that the phone is rotating and will change the view from landscape to portrait accordingly.

The challenge different screen sizes offer is simple: your design must be flexible, stretching to meet the correct proportions for the screen on which it is presented. You will see, as you read further, how this is accomplished with each of the frameworks we will work with.

An interesting challenge that smart phones provide designers is resolution. For many years web designers have been told that they can keep their web graphics set to 72 DPI (dots per inch). During 2010 this changed. First Apple and Google added functionality that allows for hi-resolution images to be added to apps and web pages. The reason for this is related to how we use our phones. Typically, you hold your phone about 8 to 12 inches from your face. Your eye can see the detail you will miss on a monitor. Top-end devices now have DPI resolution far in excess of 240 DPI (the iPhone 4 has a DPI of 334 that is branded as "Retina Display"). The result is close to print-quality graphics on your phone. Incredible and beautiful. The challenge this offers is that images that are higher in resolution are much larger in file size, as shown in the comparison between iPhone 3GS and iPhone 4 in Figure 1.7.

Desktop and laptop computers have an input model of a mouse and keyboard. Both of these inputs are very precise. The primary input device for your smart phone is your finger (if you are lucky, you have eight and two thumbs versus the one mouse a computer has).

A digit is not precise. Apple's human user interface manual suggests that buttons that you tap with your finger are 44×44

iPhone 3G Ⓢ

iPhone 4

Figure 1.7 Retina display quality on iPhone 4.

pixels at a minimum. When your screen size is only 320×480, you can see how much space you must provide for buttons tapped with a finger.

A key element that is supported across leading smart phone manufacturers is support for HTML standards. HTML5 is a great buzzword (throw it in the same group as dHTML, Web 2.0, Ajax, Cloud, etc.) that means a lot to a lot of people. HTML5 even comes with its own logo, as shown in Figure 1.8. At its core, HTML5 is a new set of HTML, elements and attributes tags in other words. For the most part, the new tags are designed to make blocking content on your web pages easier. Some tags, such as VIDEO, AUDIO, and CANVAS, add rich media solutions that allow you to add standards-based video and audio and rich Flash-like animation.

Just from this list you can see that mobile web development offers many challenges and opportunities you do not experience on a laptop. Do not think that coming to the mobile platform is the same as desktop. The customer experience is simply too different.

Figure 1.8 HTML5 logo.

The Leading Mobile Web Browsers

Today, two companies dominate browser use for smart phones: Google and Apple. It would be fair to say that close to 99% of all mobile web traffic comes from these two platforms.

Apple's Mobile Safari and Android's web browser are both built using WebKit as a foundation. This does not mean they are both equal. For instance, Mobile Safari has supported SVG graphics since version 1.0 whereas Android did not start support for SVG until the release of Honeycomb (3.0).

The two browsers enjoy huge support for a simple reason: they are the default browsers installed on the hardware.

Android does allow you to install additional web browsers but adoption rates are very low. Apple takes things one step further and prohibits additional web browsers from being submitted to the App Store.

Fortunately both browsers do have great support for modern web technologies allowing you to deliver amazing web experiences to your customers.

Additional Web Browsers

Mobile Safari and Android are not the only browsers in town. In addition, there are:

- Mobile Firefox (known as Fennec)
- Mobile Opera
- Chrome OS
- Mercury

Figure 1.9 Mobile Firefox (code name Fennec) running on an HTC Windows 6 phone.

Mobile Firefox is a port of Firefox 3.6 for the mobile platform. Currently it has limited support on Nokia Maemo phones, but there is a beta release for Android and Windows Phone 6, as shown in Figure 1.9.

Outside of the default browsers that come with Android and iOS, Opera Mobile is the most popular browser. Opera has been creating a mobile version of its browser since 2000, with each major release supporting almost all the same features as its desktop version. The current release has broad support for HTML5. Figure 1.10 shows Opera running on an HP iPAQ.

Opera Mobile runs on many platforms including Android, Windows Mobile, Maemo, and Symbian. The following phones all ship with Opera Mobile installed:

Figure 1.10 Opera browser running on an iPAQ.

- Nokia N90
- Sony Ericsson P1
- Sony Ericsson XPERIA X1
- HTC Touch Viva
- HTC Touch Diamond
- HTC Touch Diamond2
- HTC Touch Pro
- HTC Touch Pro2
- HTC Touch HD
- HTC HD2
- Meizu M8
- Creative Zii
- Samsung i900 Omnia
- Samsung i8000 Omnia II
- Motorola ROKR E6

While Opera is still a niche player on the desktop, it is a major player in the mobile arena.

The final mobile browser worth considering as you design you web pages is Chrome OS. Google is performing a strange development cycle between Android and Chrome OS. If you did not know, you would think that they compete with one another. Chrome OS is built on top of Google's Chrome web browser. Google has confirmed that Chrome OS will be installed on netbooks but Google has not declared where else it will be installed.

HTML5 in Mobile Websites

The next section dives deep into HTML5. HTML5 is an emerging standard that is the most dramatic evolution of web development standards in more than a decade. HTML5, however, has come to mean a lot more than just a new set of tags. The term now encompasses a whole set of technologies that include:

- HTML5 elements
- CSS3
- New graphic control (PNG, SVG, and CANVAS)
- Enhanced JavaScript
- Web APIs

There is even more. Amazingly, mobile browsers are ahead of desktop browsers in support for these technologies. All of the following technologies will work on Android, iOS, WebOS, and BlackBerry 6. You will need to wait for 2011 summer release of HTML5 support in Windows Phone 7 to support HTML5.

New HTML5 Elements

The blocking of content in HTML is traditionally accomplished using either complex tables or the infamous DIV element. HTML5 introduces several new elements that allow you to easily insert blocks of content into the page. Conveniently, these new elements have names that identify what the block of content accomplishes:

- HEADER
- SECTION
- ARTICLE
- ASIDE
- FOOTER
- NAV

The role of the new page layout elements is to better describe specific parts of a document. Think of the new tags as behaving in a similar way to how you approach writing a document in Microsoft Word. A typical Word document is built up of sections of content that can be separated in paragraphs, sidebars, and header and footer sections.

Blocking Content

There are few ways in HTML4 to define content. The most common is to use the P element to identify the start and end of a paragraph, or the DIV element to identify the start and end of a section of content. Both do not adequately describe the content. You can see blocking applied to most web pages.

With HTML5 a new element, the SECTION element, clearly identifies a block of content. This method is called block-level semantics. With HTML5 there are several elements that block content:

- SECTION
- ARTICLE
- HEADER
- FOOTER
- ASIDE

- FIGURE
- NAV

The new names for each of these elements identify the type of content they block on a page.

Using the SECTION Element

The SECTION element is part of a new set of elements that describe the content on a page. You can think of the SECTION element as enclosing a significant part of a page, in the same way that a chapter in a book is a significant section of the book. An example of the SECTION element follows.

```
<SECTION>
<ARTICLE>
<P>Nulla facilisis egestas nulla id rhoncus. Duis eget
diam nisi, quis sagittis nulla. Fusce lacinia pharetra
dui, a rhoncus sapien egestas.</P>
</ARTICLE>
<ARTICLE>
<P>Lorem ipsum dolor sit amet, consectetur adipiscing
elit. Nunc vehicula ipsum sit amet eros adipiscing
volutpat. Sed gravida urna vel sapien commodo pretium.</P>
</ARTICLE>
<UL>
<LI>Praesent ut sapien quam.</LI>
<LI>Aliquam erat volutpat.</LI>
</UL>
</SECTION>
```

You can see clearly that the two paragraphs, wrapped in the P element, and the two bullet points are part of the same content wrapped in the SECTION element.

The SECTION element is an efficient way to organize content in your code.

Using the ARTICLE Element

The ARTICLE element is used to clearly identify content in a web page. Blogs are a good example where content is clearly identified. The main section of a page is the content that you can wrap using the ARTICLE element. You can have additional HTML elements included within an ARTICLE. The following blog from *http://blog.whatwg.org/* is an example that shows how you can use the ARTICLE element in HTML.

```
<ARTICLE>
<H1>Spelling HTML5</H1>
<P><TIME>September 10th, 2009</TIME> by Henri
Sivonen</P>
<P>What's the right way to spell "HTML5"? The short
answer is: "HTML5" (without a space).</P>
</ARTICLE>
```

More than one ARTICLE can be added to a page. You should think of the ARTICLE element as a tool that logically breaks up content. Similar content separated by the ARTICLE element can be contained within a SECTION element.

Using the HEADER and FOOTER Elements

The top and bottom of a page created with Microsoft Word or any other word processing software is a place reserved for the header and footer information page. This includes page number, copyright notice, and other details. Web pages are no different. Header and footer information is found on most web pages.

You can see the use of the header on the page in the following HTML example. It contains the Focal Press logo, the element line, high-level links, and a search box. HTML5 allows this area of content to be clearly identified as either a header or a footer using the new HEADER and FOOTER elements.

For instance, a HEADER for Focal Press would look like the following.

```
<HEADER>
<SECTION><a href="/"><img src="/images/fplogo.png"
border="none" alt="Focal Press logo" title="Focal Press
Home"/></a> learn | master | create</b>SECTION>
    <NAV>
    <ul><li><a title="Digital Imaging and Photography"
class="first" href="/photography.aspx">Photography</a>
</li><li><a title="Production, Postproduction, and Motion
Graphics" href="/film_video.aspx">Film &amp; Video</a></
li><li><a title="Animation, 3D, and Games" href=
"/animation_3d.aspx">Animation &amp; 3D</a></li><li>
<a title="Audio Engineering and Music Technology" href=
"/audio.aspx">Audio</a></li><li><a title="Broadcast
    and Digital Media" href="/broadcast.aspx">Broadcast
</a></li><li><a title="Theatre and Live Performance" href=
"/theatre.aspx">Theatre</a></li><li><a class="offsite last"
href="http://www.elsevierdirect.com/imprint.jsp?iid=100001"
    >Bookstore </a></li> </ul></NAV>
    </HEADER>
```

The FOOTER section to a page is also viewed on most web pages. An example FOOTER in HTML5 will look as follows:

```
<FOOTER>
<P>Copyright © 2011 Focal Press, Inc.</P>
</FOOTER>
```

Unlike normal page layout, the HEADER and FOOTER are not exclusive to just the head and foot of a web page. You can have a header and footer placed around the ARTICLE or SECTION element if those pieces require specific header and footer content.

Using the ASIDE Element

The role of the ASIDE element is to describe content that is related to but is not part of the main content on the web page. You can think of the ASIDE element as fitting the role of a sidebar reference or an aside found in books and articles. The following example shows how the ASIDE element can be used with the ARTICLE element.

```
<ARTICLE>
<P>Lorem ipsum dolor sit amet, consectetur adipiscing
elit. Vivamus sed eros at metus pulvinar convallis id quis
purus. Sed lacinia condimentum viverra.</P>
<ASIDE>
<H1>What is Lorem Ipsum?</H1>
<P>Lorem Ipsum is simply dummy text of the printing and
typesetting industry.</P>
</ASIDE>
</ARTICLE>
```

The main content of the page and a support aside can be clearly separated using the ASIDE element.

Apply formatting, using CSS, to visually show where the ASIDE is on the screen.

Using the FIGURE Element

Inserting images into a web page is common practice. Identifying the image and supporting text as a figure is much more difficult. The FIGURE element clearly identifies an image and supporting description as being part of a set. This set is called a figure group. As with many of the previous new HTML5 elements, the FIGURE element is a method of blocking related content with itself.

```
<FIGURE>
<LEGEND>Figure 12. Using the FIGURE element
</LEGEND>
<IMG alt="The FIGURE element is another example
of block semantics in HTML5" src="figure_element.jpg"
border="0" height="140" width="240" />
</FIGURE>
```

The FIGURE element has an additional element you can use within it. The LEGEND element identifies the text that is to be associated with the image. The FIGURE element can be used multiple times on a page. The Border attribute is deprecated but it is still used by most browsers.

Using the NAV Element

The final HTML5 blocking element is NAV. Navigation is important to any website. The role of the NAV element is to clearly identify groups of links that when grouped together form navigation.

Navigation can take many different roles on a single web page. The different types of content that can be grouped together as navigation include, but are not limited to, the following:

- Top-level links typically found in the top-right corner of a web page
- Links that move you through data such as "Next" and "Previous"
- Links found in the footer of a web page

The following is an example of navigation grouped using the NAV element.

```
<NAV>
  <a href="/home.html">Home</a> | <a href="aboutUs.
html">About Us</a> | <a href="contactUs.html">Contact Us</a>
</NAV>
```

Of all the blocking elements in HTML5, the NAV element is one of the easiest to understand: the NAV element is used to define a section of HTML for navigation on the page.

Using CSS3

Figure 1.11 jQuery Mobile leverages CSS3 to manage the presentation of content.

Tags are used in HTML5 to place and organize content at a level that is descriptive. This does not mean that the page will look good. Presentation of content on the page is controlled using Cascading Style Sheets Level 3, or CSS3, in HTML5.

Using CSS to describe how your page should look, however, is not new. The technology was first introduced in 1997 and is now, in HTML5, in its third major release, named CSS3. The good news is that all CSS1 and CSS2 standards are fully supported by popular web browsers.

For mobile web design you will use CSS to format your web pages. There are good reasons why you want to do this. The first, and most important, is that CSS is a tool that allows you to easily apply page styling techniques to a whole website from one or more shared documents. This means you can quickly change the visual layout of a page, selection of pages, or your entire site.

The second is that Apple has GPU accelerated support for CSS. What this means is that CSS simply runs faster. Animations, rounded corners, embedded fonts, and transforms all look great on the iPhone. The powerful new Nvidia and Qualcomm chipsets appearing in most smart phones really give presentation in your web pages an edge. The result is that you can use CSS to design native app-like solutions without having to write native code. Just CSS.

In a later article you will see how jQuery Mobile enables you to build stunning solutions, with CSS3 playing a major role in the presentation. Figure 1.11 shows a website that uses CSS3 in jQuery Mobile to build a website that looks like a native application on the iPhone.

This section will not go into detail about CSS creation and development. For a more detailed analysis of CSS3 in HTML5, check out the book *HTML5: Designing Rich Internet Applications* (David, 2010).

Designing Your Web Page with CSS

CSS is much easier to master than more complex parts of HTML5 such as Local Data Storage, Geolocation, and JavaScript. The basic premise for all CSS is that you have a definition that requires a value. For instance, if you want to define the size of a particular font, you write the correct CSS definition (font-size) and place a value. Here is the code:

```
font-size: 60px;
```

There are four rules you must follow:
1. Use a valid CSS definition.
2. Place a colon after the definition.
3. Add a valid value for the definition.
4. Complete the statement with a semicolon.
    Follow these four rules and you are golden.

For basic CSS manipulation there are some great tools you can use. Adobe's Dreamweaver and Microsoft's Expression Web both support CSS2 design definition. Both of these tools are offer visual editors you can easily use to write CSS. Unfortunately your choices drop significantly when you start to look for more advanced CSS3 tools. This is in part due to the rapid development of CSS3. Check out visualizetheweb.com for the latest information on CSS3 tools.

When CSS was first released in 1997 there were about a dozen or so definitions you could use to control visual aspects such as font size, color, and background color. Now you have hundreds of different definitions that can be used extensively with any element on the screen.

Controlling Display with CSS

One of the easiest places to start learning how to use CSS definitions is through font control. CSS1 and CSS2 support nine different definitions within the font family. They are:
- Font-family
- Font-size
- Color
- Text-shadow
- Font-weight
- Font-style
- Font-variant
- Text-transform
- Text-decoration

The font-family definition allows you to select a font for your design. Here is how you write the definition:

```
font-family: Arial;
```

The challenge you have in using the font-family definition is that the number of fonts you can select from is limited to the fonts installed on the device viewing your web page. Web browsers and operating systems install a core set of fonts that you can use in your designs. The list of fonts you have available that are "web safe" includes the following:

- Arial/Helvetica
- Times New Roman/Times
- Courier New/Courier
- Verdana
- Georgia
- Comic Sans MS
- Trebuchet MS
- Arial Black
- Impact
- Palatino
- Garamond
- Bookman
- Avant Garde

This list is not very exhaustive and you run into issues where the fonts will not match. For instance, you may select the font Tahoma and it will look great on Windows Phone 7 but will not look the same on the iPhone. Often you will find that there are similar fonts on devices, but they simply have different names. For instance, you can select the following font family:

```
font-family: "Courier New", Courier, monospace;
```

This collection of fonts will allow the text to be presented correctly no matter the system viewing the page. In this instance, "Courier New" is the Windows Phone name for "Courier" on iOS. Monospace is a Unix/Linux equivalent that you will find on Android.

Here is a collection of safe font-family names you can use:

- Arial, Arial, Helvetica, sans serif
- Arial Black, Arial Black, Gadget, sans serif
- Comic Sans MS, Comic Sans MS, cursive
- Courier New, Courier New, Courier, monospace
- Georgia, Georgia, serif
- Impact, Impact, Charcoal, sans serif
- Lucida Console, Monaco, monospace
- Lucida Sans Unicode, Lucida Grande, sans serif
- Palatino Linotype, Book Antiqua, Palatino, serif
- Tahoma, Geneva, sans serif
- Times New Roman, Times, serif

- Trebuchet MS, Helvetica, sans serif
- Verdana, Verdana, Geneva, sans serif
- Wingdings, Zapf Dingbats (Wingdings, Zapf Dingbats)

Embedding Fonts Using CSS3

A way to get around the problems of creating font-family lists is to embed the font directly into your CSS. CSS3 finally allows you to do this across your web browsers. The technology for font embedding, however, is not new. Netscape Navigator 4 was the first web browser that allowed you to support font embedding using a plug-in technology called TrueDoc by Bitstream. To compete with Navigator 4, Microsoft released a "me too" technology called Embedded Open Type in the Windows version of Internet Explorer 4.

As you might expect, HTML5 has driven new technologies to enable true font embedding. Three standards are now recommended to embed fonts. They are:
- TrueType
- Scalable Vector Graphic Fonts
- WOFF

Embedding a font into your CSS document is now very easy. Figure 1.12 shows Google's Web Font directory of free HTML5 web fonts you can use now.

To embed a font into a web page you need only two things: the font file and definition in CSS linking to the font.

The font myCustomFont.ttf is being used in the CSS code below.

You need to create a new font-family in your CSS document that links to the TrueType font. The following CSS code shows, in line 2, where you can create a new font-family called "myCustomFont" and, in line 3, you are linking to the font and identifying the type of font.

Figure 1.12 Free fonts from Google you can use on your website.

```
@font-face{
font-family: 'myCustomFont';
src: url('MYCUSTOMFONT.ttf') format('truetype');
}
```

You now have a new font-family that you can reference in your normal CSS. Here, a P element is being formatted using the new font-family:

```
p {
text-align: center;
font-family: 'myCustomFont';
font-size:3cm;
}
```

Now your web pages will display the embedded font correctly no matter what web browser is viewing your design. Font freedom has finally come to the web!

Sizing Your Fonts with CSS Units of Measurement

After selecting a font-family for your text you will also want to select the size of the font. By default, all web browsers have a preinstalled definition for a standard font size. This font size is usually 12 pt. You can use this as a size for your fonts as they appear on the screen using the following CSS font-size definition:

```
Font-size:medium;
```

If you want your font to appear smaller or larger on the screen you can use the following sizes for your fonts:
- Xx-small (approximately 7.5 pt)
- X-small (approximately 9 pt)
- Small (approximately 10 pt)
- Medium (approximately 12 pt)
- Large (approximately 14 pt)
- X-large (approximately 18 pt)
- Xx-large (approximately 24 pt)
- Smaller
- Larger

Each of these font sizes are relative to the core browser defaulted font size. If the person who owns the web browser has changed that default then the sizes will dynamically change.

As a designer you are limited by the default font size list. The good news is that CSS allows you to leverage units of measurement to add precise size to your font. The following are all valid CSS units of measurement you can use.
- Cm: Centimeter
- In: Inch
- Mm: Millimeter
- Pc: Pica (1 p = 12 pts)
- Pt: Point (1 pt = 1/72 inch)
- Px: Pixels
- Rem: Font size of the root element

Using these different font sizes, the following styles are all valid:

```
.default {
        font-family: "Segoe UI", Tahoma, Geneva, Verdana;
        font-size: medium;
}
.px {
        font-family: "Segoe UI", Tahoma, Geneva, Verdana;
        font-size: 15px;
}
```

```
.cm {
        font-family: "Segoe UI", Tahoma, Geneva, Verdana;
        font-size: .5cm;
}
.mm {
        font-family: "Segoe UI", Tahoma, Geneva, Verdana;
        font-size: 2mm;
}
.inch {
        font-family: "Segoe UI", Tahoma, Geneva, Verdana;
        font-size: .25in;
}
.pica {
        font-family: "Segoe UI", Tahoma, Geneva, Verdana;
        font-size: 2pc;
}
.point {
        font-family: "Segoe UI", Tahoma, Geneva, Verdana;
        font-size: 10pt;
}
.rem {
        font-family: "Segoe UI", Tahoma, Geneva, Verdana;
        font-size: 1rem;
}
```

These font styles are applied to the following HTML:

```
<p class="default">In hac habitasse platea dictumst.</p>
<p class="px">Lorem ipsum dolor sit amet, consectetur
adipiscing elit. Etiam accumsan convallis odio, vitae
semper mi pretium laoreet. </p>
<p class="cm">In vestibulum, ipsum consectetur cursus
porttitor, mi tellus euismod purus, ac egestas nisl
risus ac risus. Suspendisse a nisi mi, nec rutrum nisi.
Suspendisse pretium aliquet convallis. </p>
<p class="mm">Aliquam sollicitudin elementum est,
commodo gravida lorem imperdiet ac. </p>
<p class="inch">In hac habitasse platea dictumst
. </p>
<p class="pica">Donec rhoncus turpis vitae risus
commodo ac mollis ligula aliquam. Donec in mi arcu, id
vulputate turpis. </p>
<p class="point">Nullam nunc dui, euismod vel lobortis
nec, suscipit non velit. </p>
<p class="rem">Aliquam ornare, nibh eget facilisis
lobortis, ligula velit suscipit sem, id condimentum est
turpis ut magna. </p>
```

Figure 1.13 shows you how these fonts are presented in your mobile browser.

Figure 1.13 The @ font-face is used to embed fonts in the above web page.

CSS3 Color Control

As with size, color has many different units of measurement. The default for web design is hexadecimal, a combination of six letters and numbers. CSS3 provides you a much broader palette of colors to choose from that include the following:

- Color Name: You can use a name for color such as Brown, Black, Red, or even Cyan.
- Full Hexadecimal: A hexadecimal value comprised of six alphanumeric values.
- Short Hexadecimal: A hexadecimal value comprised of three alphanumeric values.
- RGB: A combination of red, green, and blue values.
- RGBA: A combination of red, green, and blue values with a transparency value (Alpha).
- HSL: A combination of hue, saturation, and lightness.
- HSLA: A combination of hue, saturation, and lightness with a transparency value (Alpha).

The following CSS uses these values to show how you can create the color red different ways:

```
.name {
color: red;
}
.fullHexVersion {
color: #FF0000;
}
.shortHexVersion {
color: #F00;
}
.rgb {
color: rgb(255,0,0);
}
.rgba {
color: rgba(255,0,0,100);
}
.hsl {
color: hsl(0%, 100%, 50%);
}
.hsla {
color: hsl(0%, 100%, 50%, 100%);
}
```

These different values are used in different places within the design community.

Adding Drop Shadow Text Effects

Love them or hate them, you cannot get away from the handy design technique of drop shadows. CSS3 now supports drop shadow effects, and they are very easy to add to your designs.

There are four elements that you can use to control the drop shadow definition. They are:

- Horizontal-offset (length, required)
- Vertical-offset (length, required)
- Blur-radius (length, optional)
- Shadow-color (color, optional)

The following CSS definition is an example of the use of the drop shadow, illustrated in Figure 1.14.

```
.dropShadow {
        font-family: "Segoe UI", Tahoma, Geneva, Verdana;
        font-size: 3cm;
        color: #CC3300;
        text-shadow: 0.25em 0.25em 2px #999;
}
```

The effect draws a light gray drop shadow with a slight blur.

Different colors and units of measurement can be used with the drop shadow effect. The following CSS definition uses pixels and RGBA for the measurement and color.

```
.transparentDropShadow {
        font-family: "Segoe UI", Tahoma, Geneva, Verdana;
        font-size: 25px;
        color: rgba(255,0,0,1);
        text-shadow: 5px 5px 5px rgba(0, 0, 0, 0.5);
}
```

Figure 1.14 A CSS3 drop shadow.

Finally, you can use the drop shadow effect to force a "cut out" effect with your text. Apply the following CSS to text on the screen:

```
.cutout {
        font-family: "Segoe UI", Tahoma, Geneva, Verdana;
        font-size: 3cm;
        color: white;
        text-shadow: 0em 0em 2em black;
}
```

Figure 1.15 demonstrates the effect of the drop shadow as a cut out.

Working with Columns in CSS3

A challenge for any web page is to create content that is split over two or more columns on the page. Creating columns often requires using complex tables structured together. Though not strictly part of the text family of CSS definitions, the new multicolumn layout is best when used with text on the screen.

The goal of the multicolumn definition is to allow your content to be spread evenly over two or more columns. There are three parts to a column layout:

- The number of columns
- The gap between the columns
- Column design (optional)

Figure 1.15 The CSS3 drop shadow effect can also be used as a cut-out effect.

The following CSS demonstrates how you can set up multicolumns to display in WebKit-enabled browsers.

```
.simple {
        font-family: "Segoe UI", Tahoma, Geneva, Verdana;
        font-size: 12px;
        color:#444;
        text-align: justify;
        -moz-column-count: 2;
        -moz-column-gap: 1em;
        -webkit-column-count: 2;
        -webkit-column-gap: 1em;
        }
```

In this example, the column-count is two and the gap is 1 em. Figure 1.16 shows how this is displayed in your web browser.

You can add a column design between each column. The structure is:

```
-moz-column-rule: 1px solid #222;
-webkit-column-rule: 1px solid #222;
```

Figure 1.16 A simple two-column layout using CSS3.

For each column design you can identify the width, border style, and color. You can use the standard measurement and color CSS formatting. You can choose from the following border styles:

- None
- Hidden
- Dotted
- Dashed
- Solid
- Double
- Groove
- Ridge
- Inset
- Outset

Additional elements, such as the IMG, can be used with text content in the column layout. Figure 1.17 illustrates a complex use of a multicolumn layout.

Figure 1.17 A complex three-column layout.

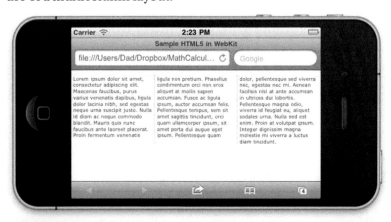

The CSS to create this layout is:

```
.complex {
        font-family: "Segoe UI", Tahoma, Geneva, Verdana;
        font-size: 1.2pc;
        color:#444;
        text-align: left;
        -moz-column-count: 3;
        -moz-column-gap: 1em;
        -moz-column-rule: 2px dotted #999;
        -webkit-column-count: 3;
        -webkit-column-gap: 1em;
        -webkit-column-rule: 2px dotted #999;
        }
```

The style in this column layout is applied to P element, which contains both text and an IMG element. You should experiment with columns. They are certainly much easier to use than complex tables.

Increase Your Control over Gradient Colors

Control over your use of color has increased significantly with CSS3. You saw earlier that you can use long hexadecimal, short hexadecimal, RGB, RGBA, HSL, and HSLA to have access to millions of colors. In addition to solid colors, CSS3 gives you the ability to add gradients.

You can currently create two different types of gradient: linear and radial. Figure 1.18 illustrates the two different gradient types you can create.

The gradient definition is comprised of several key elements. They are:

- Type: Either radial or linear
- Point: Two space-separated values that explain where the gradient starts (this can be achieved with a number, percentage, or by using the keywords top, bottom, left, and right)
- Radius: The radius is a number that you only need to specify when you use the radial type
- Stop: The function of the Stop value is to identify the blend strength as a percentage or number between 0 and 1 (such as .75 or 75%) and a color; you can use any CSS3 supported color

Putting all of these together will give you a gradient. Gradients can be used with the following definitions:

```
background-image
border-image
list-style-image
content property
```

Figure 1.18 CSS3 allows you to add gradient colors.

The following example adds a gradient that goes from red-to-orange-to-orange-to-yellow:

```
body {
    background-image: -webkit-gradient(linear, left top,
left bottom, from(red), to(yellow), color-stop(0.5, orange),
color-stop(0.5, orange));}
```

As you can see, the gradient is substituting an image in the background-image definition. The first definition identifies the gradient as linear. The next definition explains that the gradient is going to go from top to bottom. The two elected colors are red and yellow. The stop function has the colors blending halfway through to orange.

A radial gradient is completed in a similar way. The following adds a radial gradient that moves from red-to-orange-to-yellow:

```
body {
    background-image: -webkit-gradient(radial, 45 45, 15, 100
100, 250, from(red), to(yellow), color-stop(50%, orange));}
```

In this instance, the numbers following the radial declaration determine the shape of the radius. The first two numbers dictate the angle of the ellipse in degrees. The third number dictates the size of the inner circle. The fourth and fifth numbers dictate the position of the gradient (left and top). The final number dictates the final size of the radius.

Multiple Background Objects

You quickly run into limitations when you can use only one background image. With CSS3 you can now run multiple background images. Any element that supports the background-image definition now supports multiple background images. Using background images is very easy. You can start by listing the images you want to use. Take for instance the following:

```
background-image:
    url(http://upload.wikimedia.org/wikipedia/commons/3/36/
Team_Singapore_fireworks_display_from_Singapore_Fireworks_
Festival_2006.jpg), url(http://upload.wikimedia.org/
wikipedia/commons/b/b2/OperaSydney-Fuegos2006-342289398.
jpg);
```

You can specify where you want each background to appear on the screen using the background-position definition. The definition is paired for the position of the background.

```
background-position: bottom left, top right;
```

Figure 1.19 Multiple backgrounds.

Figure 1.19 shows the end result.

As you might expect, you can mix gradients and multiple background images together. The following CSS blends a radial gradient with two background images.

```
<html>
<head>
<title>Multiple Backgrounds</title>
  <style>
  body {
    background-image:
    url(http://upload.wikimedia.org/wikipedia/
commons/3/36/Team_Singapore_fireworks_display_from_
Singapore_Fireworks_Festival_2006.jpg),
      url(http://upload.wikimedia.org/wikipedia/
commons/b/b2/OperaSydney-Fuegos2006-342289398.jpg),
-webkit-gradient(radial, 45 45, 15, 100 100, 250, from(gold),
to(magenta), color-stop(50%, black));
    background-repeat: no-repeat;
    background-position: bottom left, top right;
      background-color:black;}
  </style>
</head>
<body>
</body>
</html>
```

Adding Rounded Corners to Layers

Adding rounded corners is not a new technique for the web. You see it all the time when you look at websites. The effect, however, is created through using images and tables to create the illusion of rounded corners. Adding images to the pages ensures that the page takes longer to load and makes modifying the page later more complex.

A simpler approach is to use the proposed Corner-Radius CSS definition that is currently supported in Mobile Firefox, Mobile Safari 3.0, and the Android web browser. The Corner-Radius definition is a line you can add to your CSS style. The following HTML code has a style embedded that changes the presentation of the block of text to have rounded corners with a heavy, black outline:

```
<p style="-moz-border-radius: 10px;-webkit-border-radius:
10px;border: 4px solid #FF0000;">Lorem ipsum dolor sit amet,
consectetur adipiscing elit. Nam porta, lacus in cursus
cursus, justo purus fringilla nisi, quis cursus urna velit vel
felis. Nulla ac mi. Phasellus sodales dui vel tortor. Praesent
dignissim. Vestibulum vulputate nibh rutrum purus. Nulla ante.
Sed porta. Vestibulum commodo, mi nec tincidunt laoreet, urna
risus ornare libero, in imperdiet sapien enim vel nisi.</p>
```

Your content will now look like Figure 1.20 on your web page.

Figure 1.20 Rounded corners in your mobile site.

As you can see, the block of text now has a solid red line with rounded corners. It is this style description that controls the size of the radius, not an image. You can then easily modify the description as shown here:

```
-moz-border-radius: 10px
-webkit-border-radius: 10px
```

The standard is currently only in proposal stage and has not been adopted by all web browsers. For this reason, you need to add two border-radius style descriptions: one for Firefox (-moz-border-radius) and one for WebKit (-webkit-border-radius). Changing the value of the border-radius will change the size of the border. For instance:

```
Border-radius: 15 px
Border-radius: 25 px
Border-radius: 45 px
```

As you increase the border radius, you will also have to add additional styles, such as padding, to ensure that your border does not cut through your text as is shown in the example of border-radius: 45 px. Here is how you can add padding to manage your style.

```
<p style="-moz-border-radius: 45px;-webkit-border-
radius: 45px;border: 4px solid #FF0000;padding: 12px;">
Lorem ipsum dolor sit amet, consectetur adipiscing elit. Nam
porta, lacus in cursus cursus, justo purus fringilla nisi,
quis cursus urna velit vel felis. Nulla ac mi. Phasellus
sodales dui vel tortor. Praesent dignissim. Vestibulum
vulputate nibh rutrum purus. Nulla ante. Sed porta.
Vestibulum commodo, mi nec tincidunt laoreet, urna risus
ornare libero, in imperdiet sapien enim vel nisi.</p>
```

Without using complex images or tables, you have created a series of tabs that can be easily managed through your CSS and HTML.

Dazzling Your Audience with CSS3 Animation

CSS3 continues to expand what you can visually accomplish in your web pages. Animation is now also available to you as the design. Animation is split into two key parts: transitions and transforms.

Transitions control the change of state for an element, such as text fading in or changing color; transforms control the placement of an element.

The following two sections explain how you can control these two new animation techniques in your CSS designs.

Using Transitions in CSS

The transition effect is best used when you create a class and then a "hover" pseudo class to illustrate when the effect is to happen (i.e., when your cursor moves over the element). The transition itself is made of three parts:

- Property: The linked property between the two classes
- Duration: How long in seconds the transition will take
- Timing-function

The timing function keywords control different types of animation sequence:

- Linear: The linear function just returns as its output the input that it received.
- Ease: The default function, ease, is equivalent to cubic-bezier (0.25, 0.1, 0.25, 1.0).
- Ease-in: The ease-in function is equivalent to cubic-bezier (0.42, 0, 1.0, 1.0).
- Ease-out: The ease-out function is equivalent to cubic-bezier (0, 0, 0.58, 1.0).
- Ease-in-out: The ease-in-out function is equivalent to cubic-bezier (0.42, 0, 0.58, 1.0).
- Cubic-bezier: Specifies a cubic-bezier curve whose P0 and P3 points are (0,0) and (1,1), respectively. The four values specify points P1 and P2 of the curve as (x1, y1, x2, y2).

The following example applies a transition effect on the color definition in the PARAGRAPH element:

```
p {
        -webkit-transition: color 2s linear;
        font-size: medium;
        font-family: Arial, Helvetica, sans-serif;
        color: #FF0000;
}
p:active {
        font-family: Arial, Helvetica, sans-serif;
        color: #0000FF;
}
```

As you select any text using the PARAGRAPH element the text will slowly change from red to blue.

The top paragraph is red, the third has transitioned to blue, and the fourth is transitioning from one color to the next. You can elect to have all the properties be selected as part of the transition by changing the property value to "ALL" as in the following example.

```
p {
        -webkit-transition: all 2s linear;
        font-size: medium;
        font-family: Arial, Helvetica, sans-serif;
        color: #FF0000;
```

```
    }
p:active {
        font-family: Arial, Helvetica, sans-serif;
        font-size: xx-large;
        color: #0000FF;
    }
```

For quick, simple animation sequences, transitions are great.

Creating Animation with CSS3

For more complex animation you will want to use the new transform settings. The following HTML and CSS style allows you to add a bouncing text block to the screen:

```
<html>
<head>
 <title>Bouncing Box example</title>
 <style type="text/css" media="screen">
  @-webkit-keyframes bounce {
   from {
   left: 0px;
   }
   to {
    left: 400px;
   }
  }
   .animation {
   -webkit-animation-name: bounce;
   -webkit-animation-duration: 2s;
   -webkit-animation-iteration-count: 4;
   -webkit-animation-direction: alternate;
   position: relative;
   left: 0px;
   }
 </style>
</head>
<body>
 <p class="animation">
  The text bounces back and forth
 </p>
</body>
</html>
```

The animation is controlled through the use of the style sheet. There are two parts you need to control. The first sets up the type of animation you want to use. Here the setting is for an animation sequence named "bounce." The animation and the movement will be from 0 px to the left 400 px:

```
@-webkit-keyframes bounce {
 from {
  left: 0px;
```

```
  }
  to {
   left: 400px;
  }
  }
```

The next step is to define what gets animated. In this example you have a CSS class associated with the "bounce" animation described earlier. There are a couple of additional settings. The duration setting controls how long each animation sequence takes to play in seconds and the count setting specifies how many times the animation plays. Together, it looks like this:

```
.animation {
 -webkit-animation-name: bounce;
 -webkit-animation-duration: 2s;
 -webkit-animation-iteration-count: 4;
 -webkit-animation-direction: alternate;
 position: relative;
 left: 0px;
```

All mobile browsers support these new animation techniques.

Using Class and Pseudo Styles

A pseudo class is a special extension to the element style definition. The most common use for pseudo classes is with the ANCHOR element. The way an ANCHOR element (the element that identifies links on a web page) is defined in CSS is as follows:

```
a {
        text-decoration: none;
        color: #0000FF;
  }
```

The ANCHOR element, however, completes several different activities. The ANCHOR element has the default style, but also can have different styles when the link is being selected, when the link has been visited, and when you move your cursor over the link. Each of these different activities can be identified with pseudo classes. The following shows the pseudo class for a link that has been visited:

```
a:visited {
        color: #FF0000;
  }
```

The ANCHOR element is listed first in your style document and is followed by a colon with the special pseudo class name called "visited." In your web page, the visited link will now have a different color.

The ANCHOR element has four pseudo classes: link, active, hover, and visited. The following style shows how you can define these four pseudo classes.

```
a{
        color: #0000FF;
}
a:link {
        text-decoration: none;
}
a:active {
        text-decoration: line-through;
}
a:visited {
        color: #FF0000;
}
```

The result is that you can now control the different actions of the ANCHOR tag.

CSS3 introduces additional pseudo class styles you can use. The complete list is:

- Active: The active element
- Focus: The element with focus
- Visited: A visited link
- Hover: The state when your cursor is over a link (this feature of CSS will *not* work on mobile devices)
- Link: An unvisited link
- Disabled: The state of an element when it has been disabled
- Enabled: The state of an element when it has been enabled
- Checked: A form element that has been checked
- Selection: When a user selects a range of content on the page
- Lang: The designer can choose which language is used for the style
- Nth-child(n): An element that is a specified child of the first sibling
- Nth-last-child(n): An element that is a specified child of the last sibling
- First-child: The first use of an element on the page
- Last-child: The last use of an element on the page
- Only-child: The only use of a element on the page

Media Definition Control

As we discussed earlier, different devices have different screen sizes. To help you, CSS3 has a final trick up its sleeve.

The media definition in CSS allows you to identify different styles for different media types. Originally defined in CSS2, the CSS3 expands the functionality of the CSS2 version to allow you to specify any type of device.

The easiest place to use the media definition is right when you link to a CSS document in the head of the web page. Typically you will write the following code to link to a CSS document:

```
<link rel="stylesheet" type="text/css" href="style.css">
```

The media definition now allows you to specify a style to be associated with a device. Take for instance the following CSS link reference to two styles documents.

```
<link rel="stylesheet" type="text/css" media="screen"
href="screen.css">
    <link rel="stylesheet" type="text/css" media="print"
href="print.css">
```

The first link uses the media definition to target a CSS document from the computer screen. The second CSS document targets how data is presented when it is printed. Using this technique you can create two different presentation styles using the same content. One style is used for screen presentation and the other for print. Following is a list of the media names you can use:

- All: Suitable for all devices
- Braille: Intended for Braille tactile feedback devices
- Embossed: Intended for paged Braille printers
- Handheld: Intended for handheld devices (typically small screen, limited bandwidth)
- Print: Intended for paged material and for documents viewed on-screen in print preview mode
- Projection: Intended for projected presentations; for example, projectors
- Screen: Intended primarily for color computer screens
- Speech: Intended for speech synthesizers
- TTY: Intended for media using a fixed-pitch character grid (such as teletypes, terminals, or portable devices with limited display capabilities)
- TV: Intended for television-type devices (low resolution, color, limited-scrollability screens, sound available)

Having the names is great, but it does not help when there are so many different devices coming on to the market with different screen resolutions. To help with this you can modify the media type to look for screen resolutions and deliver the appropriate style sheet. Using the property device-width you can specify a style sheet for a specific width.

```
<link rel="stylesheet" type="text/css" media="(device-
width: 320px)" href="iphoneClassic.css">
```

Using CSS you can dynamically change the presentation of the content to best suit the device accessing the content.

Graphical Control with Bitmap, SVG, and CANVAS Elements

Tags are used in HTML5 to place and organize content at a level that is descriptive. This does not mean that the page will look good.

There are times, however, when you need to present graphics, too. Typically, HTML has provided support for pixel-based images only in JPG and GIF image format. With HTML5, you can now create mathematically generated images. The new formats are Scalable Vector Graphics, SVG, and CANVAS. The difference between the two is that SVG is an XML-based language that describes how an image should be displayed in 2D constructs. The CANVAS tag also describes 2D images, but it does so using JavaScript. The CANVAS tag also allows you to easily integrate interactivity within it using JavaScript.

Working with Bitmap Images on the Web

The web is not a friendly place for the designer. For many years you have been limited in the number of the file formats you can use. There are two predominant file formats used on the web for creating graphics: JPG and GIF.

JPEG, PNG, and GIF image formats are raster images created from pixels of individual color. Each has positives and negatives. JPEG images are an open standard managed by the Joint Photographers Expert Group. The JPEG file format allows you to create photo-realistic images. A great place to go to view millions of JPEG images is Yahoo's Flickr, as shown in Figure 1.21. A JPEG image is identified with either a JPEG or JPG extension .

The second file format used widely on the Internet is GIF, Graphics Interchange Format. Unlike JPEG, which supports millions of colors, the GIF file format only allows you to create images that support a color palette of 256 colors. On the face of it, the GIF format appears to be inferior to the JPEG format. However, the GIF format does have two features the JPEG format does not: setting transparency as a color and sequencing a series of images together to play back as a simple animation. It also handles solid colors more effectively.

Both JPEG and GIF image formats, however, are now being superseded by a more sophisticated image format: PNG.

Portable Network Graphics, PNG, are a raster-based file format that gives you the best of both JPEG and GIF and a little more. PNG image will support 32-byte images for photo-realistic presentation. Additionally, backgrounds in PNG images can be set to be transparent, the same as GIF images.

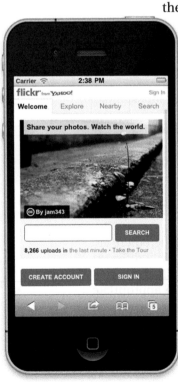

Figure 1.21 Images loaded to Flickr are in JPEG format.

While PNG, GIF, and JPEG images are all great, it is difficult to programmatically change the graphical display of the images. For instance, you cannot create a bar chart using JPEG images that change as new data comes in. HTML5 introduces two solutions that address this problem: SVG and CANVAS.

Working with CANVAS and SVG Graphics

The CANVAS HTML5 element allows you to create bitmap images programmatically using JavaScript as the designer. Through this technique complex animations and interactive solutions can be created. Google has established ChromeExperiments.com (*www.chromeexperiments. com/*) to demonstrate powerful CANVAS and JavaScript experiments.

The second technology, SVG, Scalable Vector Graphics, is a vector-based technology that enables you to create images and animation using XML syntax similar to HTML. SVG started as an Open Standard in 1999. The support for SVG started out patchy in the mobile community. For a long time, only Mobile Safari on iOS devices supported SVG. However, the release of Android 3.0 and 2.4 have changed this.

Figure 1.22 SVG graphics in iOS.

SVG is a vector-based image format very similar to native Flash drawings. This gives you a great advantage when it comes to hi-res screen displays. No matter how detailed the screen is trying to be, the image will always be crisp without affecting the size of the file. In contrast, PNG and other raster images need larger files for crisper images at high resolutions. Figure 1.22 is an SVG illustration of the official SVG logo.

Unfortunately, although CANVAS drawings do render on all mobile browsers, the processing needed by the JavaScript engine is spotty. Apple does not use GPU enhancement for CANVAS drawing, relying on an already overburdened CPU. Some Android sellers running Android 2.2 can leverage the speedy V8 JavaScript engine to speed up CANVAS redrawing. This is a problem today, but will likely be mitigated by more powerful and smarter devices coming out in 2011 and 2012.

Adding Video to Your Web Pages

Today, people will watch more than 2 billion movies on the Internet. That's right, two *billion*. Video is a big deal. Fortunately, HTML5 makes it easier for you to add video when you use a new HTML element called VIDEO, as shown in the screen shot in Figure 1.23.

Figure 1.23 Video controlled by HTML.

Mobile devices were among the first widely used devices that supported the new VIDEO element. Over the last couple of years there has been a lot of controversy over how you can use the VIDEO element. Essentially, adding video with the VIDEO element is very simple: you can use a tag in your web page with a few attributes. Here is an example:

```
<video src="mobileVideo.mp4" ></video>
```

This example links to an MPEG4-encoded video. That's it. No fussing with plug-in OBJECT tags and parameters. Just use one line to add a simple, powerful HTML5 element.

This new VIDEO element has instigated a war of words about which video format the VIDEO element should play. There are three formats jostling for votes (MPEG4, Ogg, and WebM). The good news is, the top mobile web browsers now support VIDEO. For instance, Apple's Mobile Safari for iPhone and iPad, Google's Android and Chrome OS, and Mobile Opera and Mobile Firefox all support the new HTML5 VIDEO element.

In this section, I introduce you to:
- The HTML5 VIDEO element
- The attributes used to control content within the element
- How to encode HTML5 VIDEO
- Whether or not you should be using HTML5 VIDEO in your mobile website

By the time you reach the end of this article you will be comfortable working with the new HTML5 VIDEO element in your mobile web pages.

Controlling Video with VIDEO Tags

As we've seen, adding a VIDEO element requires only one line in your HTML. The following example adds opening and closing tags for the VIDEO element. The first tag includes an SRC attribute that points to a supported HTML5 video file (in this example we're pointing to an MPEG4 video):

```
<video src="mobileVideo.mp4" ></video>
```

That's it. Additional functionality can be added using the following attributes in the VIDEO element:
- Autoplay: The video will play immediately if already downloaded in your cache (this attribute does not work on iOS devices, but does on Android)
- Controls: A simple playback head will be added with VCR-like play and pause controls
- Height and Width
- Loop: You can loop the video
- Poster: Allows you to set a placeholder image for the video

To get the most out of your video playback you'll want to use some of these attributes. For instance, if you want your video to start playing when the web page has finished loading, you should use the Autoplay attribute as follows:

```
<video src="mobileVideo.mp4" autoplay></video>
```

The video won't automatically play if you don't include it. A second useful attribute to add is the Controls attribute:

```
<video src="mobileVideo.mp4" autoplay controls></video>
```

Try viewing the Controls attribute in different mobile browsers such as Mobile Safari on the iPhone or iPad, and Android's browser—you'll notice it looks different in each browser. Each browser plays back the video differently, and each engine has its own default control style. This can make it difficult to present a video playback experience that's consistent from one browser to another.

You can override the default video playback features with some creative JavaScript and CSS.

> **Note**
> The *Autoplay* attribute doesn't work with Mobile Safari on the iPhone and iPad but will work for Android devices.

Using JavaScript to Control the VIDEO Element

JavaScript is able to control any elements in HTML. The VIDEO element is a valid, first-level element JavaScript can control. This means you can control media using your own custom controls. The following example will show you how to add a custom Play/ Pause button to your video.

Start with a blank HTML5 page:

```
<!DOCTYPE HTML>
<html>
<head>
<title>Adding Video to a Mobile App</title>
</head>
<body>
</body>
</html>
```

In the BODY section, add the VIDEO element and link to a video file:

```
<video autoplay >
<source src="mobileVideo.mp4">
</video>
```

You can see here that the video file doesn't have any attributes that control playback. You can add those controls programmatically with JavaScript. Let's start by adding the controls that play the movie:

```
<a href="#" >Play/Pause</a>
```

After the VIDEO element, add the following JavaScript:

```
<script>
  var video = document.getElementsByTagName('video')[0];
</script>
```

This script gives the VIDEO element a name you can reference. The final step is to add a script to the ANCHOR tag:

```
<a href="#" onclick="if (video.paused) video.play();
else video.pause()">Play/Pause</a>;
```

The ANCHOR element uses an on-click event to trigger an IF/ELSE JavaScript command. If the button is pressed and the video hasn't been played, then the video will start to play. Else, if the video is playing and the button is selected it will pause the video. Altogether your code will look like this:

```
<!DOCTYPE HTML>
<html>
<head>
<title>Adding Video to a Mobile App</title>
</head>
<body>
<video autoplay >
<source src="mobileVideo.mp4">
</video>
<script>
var video = document.getElementsByTagName('video')[0];
</script>
<br />
<a href="#" onclick="if (video.paused) video.play();
else video.pause()">Play/Pause</a>
</p>
</body>
</html>
```

An additional benefit of using JavaScript to control the presentation of your controls is that you can use CSS to style them. Here is a basic style applied to our video controls:

```
<!DOCTYPE HTML>
<html>
<head>
<title>Video in HTML5</title>
<style type="text/css">
a {
        font-family: Arial, sans-serif;
        font-size: large;
        text-decoration: none;
        color: #C0C0C0;
}
h1 {
```

```
                Arial, sans-serif;
                font-size: 24pt;
                color: #C0C0C0;
        }
        body {
                background-color: #000000;
        }
        </style>
        </head>
        <body>
        <h1 align="center">Video on your Mobile Device</h1>
<p align="center">
        <video autoplay >
         <source src="mobileVideo.mp4">
        </video>
         <script>
         var video = document.getElementsByTagName('video')[0];
         </script>
        <br />
         <a href="#" onclick="if (video.paused) video.play();
else video.pause()"> Play/Pause</a>
        </p>
        </body>
        </html>
```

There are other controls you can add to your VIDEO element. You can add a playback head to track where you are in the video, for example, as well as fast-forward and rewind.

Encoding Video and Audio for Web Delivery

The H.264 support, also known as MPEG4, is the video and audio format supported on your iPhone and used by many companies. Unfortunately, MPEG4 has patents that protect the technology. This has lead to confusion about whether or not you can freely use MPEG4 video in your web pages. The patent group managing MPEG4, the MPEG-LA group, has stated it will *not* charge royalties for the use of MPEG4 video embedded into web pages. Check out the comprehensive FAQ Microsoft put together here: *www.microsoft.com/windows/windowsmedia/licensing/mpeg4faq. aspx.*

The alternatives to H.264 are Theora and webM formats. Technically, H.264 is cleaner at higher resolutions (you'd have to be a videophile to see the difference), but overall the quality difference between H.264 and Theora/WebM is minimal. Ultimately, consumers of video/audio content will determine which CODEC will become the format of choice.

The challenge we face now is identifying which browser supports which video format. Table 1.1 provides a brief breakdown: As you can see, not all browsers support all video formats.

Table 1.1 Supported HTML5 Video CODECs

	MPEG4	Ogg Theora	WebM
Mobile Firefox	No	Yes	No
Chrome OS	No	Yes	Yes
Mobile Safari	Yes	No	No
Windows Phone 7	No	No	No
Mobile Opera	No	Yes	No

Creating Video in H.264 Format

Creating H.264-formatted video is relatively easy. There are dozens of products on the market that will take almost any video format and convert it to MPEG4, including Cucusoft, MP4 Convertor, and more. For Mac users, it's even easier; your copy of iMovie already supports MPEG4 format.

Creating Video in Ogg Theora and WebM Formats

There are a few tools that allow you to create Ogg Theora video. You can check out the latest solutions here: *www.theora. org/downloads/*.

The challenge to WebM as a new CODEC is support in creating WebM files. Fortunately, the group managing WebM as an Open Standard, the WebM Project, has a website with open-source tools you can use to encode video into WebM formats. Check it out at *www.webmproject.org/code*.

Ensuring Your Video Plays Back

Currently, not all mobile browsers support the same video playback. This leaves you with a thorny problem: How do you support video across all these different browsers?

Well, HTML5 has that covered. The VIDEO element allows you to add nested SOURCE elements:

```
<video autoplay controls>
<source src="sample.mp4">
<source src="sample.ogv">
<source src="sample.webm">
</video>
```

Using this technique guarantees your HTML5-compliant web browser will play back your video by selecting the first file that matches a CODEC installed on your device.

Streaming for Video Playback on Mobile Devices

In addition to controlling whether or not video will actually play on your mobile device, you also need to know whether or not the bandwidth streaming to the phone will allow the video to play back.

There are two ways you can control the playback of video: download or streaming.

Downloading files requires that the whole video is either first downloaded or, if the CODEC allows for it, will start playing back as the video is being downloaded, a feature known as progressive download. The MPEG4 format has progressive download built into the architecture. This allows for rented movies to start playing within a couple of minutes of selecting the title on your iPad. You do not need to wait for two to three hours for the whole movie to download.

Streaming is a method where the video is delivered in a series of small packets to the device. Unlike progressive download where the whole movie is downloaded to the browser cache, streaming does not leave any file on the device. The method allows for live video to be streamed to a device. The downside to streaming is that you must have a constant connection to the Internet for it to work.

Network connectivity is the largest challenge for delivering video to mobile devices. Today, four main data speeds are used to send data to a mobile device:

- WiFi
- 4G LTE
- 3G CDMA
- EDGE

The size of the screen, such as handheld or tablet, will determine what size video stream you are sending. For instance, for a phone, you can stream smaller video simply because the screen is smaller. However for a tablet device you will want to stream an HD quality video file to fill up the larger screen.

Larger video images will require faster Internet connections. Both 4G and WiFi are more than capable of streaming HD quality video. A 3G signal will be able to stream only a sub-DVD quality video, whereas EDGE, the slowest connection speed, will be able to stream only very small video images.

By default, HTML5 does not allow you to switch files as determined by network connection. Fortunately, you can use a feature built into modern web servers, such as Microsoft's Internet Information Server 7, called HTTP Live Streaming. With HTTP Live Streaming you can add a single file reference in the web page and the server can then dynamically select the appropriate video for the network bandwidth.

For HTTP Live Streaming to work, the web browser does need to understand and support the protocol. Fortunately, iOS, BlackBerry PlayBook, and Android do. It is also very likely the Windows Phone 7 will support HTTP Streaming when the browser adopts HTML5.

Applying New Web API Functionality to Your Mobile Web Pages

CSS, SVG, and Video are all great improvements to HTML5. The role for HTML5, however, is not simply to add eye-candy, but to enable developers to create applications in web browsers that are equal in performance to desktop applications. To accomplish this you need a powerful development language that gives developers the ability to create sophisticated solutions. The answer to this is JavaScript, the world's most popular programming language.

Currently, the belief is that web applications are simply not as powerful as desktop applications. The reason for this is not due to JavaScript, but the engines inside your web browser that process JavaScript. The faster a script can be processed, the more sophisticated your applications can become.

HTML5 is expanding to support application programming interfaces (APIs) that enable complex system integration inside your web page. The new APIs, such as geolocation and local data storage, are complex and require sophisticated use of JavaScript to make them work.

JavaScript is not a new technology. The roots of JavaScript go back to 1993 when Netscape Communications included a scripting technology called LiveScript with its web browser. Incorporating even a simple programming language that enables interactivity in the web browser became extremely popular.

The current release of JavaScript has dramatically matured the original LiveScript language. Unlike desktop applications that run code optimized for an operating system, JavaScript must be interpreted within a virtual machine translator running inside the web browser. This process inherently forces JavaScript solutions to run more slowly. To compensate for this, Google uses a technology called V8 that dramatically improves the processing of JavaScript code in Android 2.2. Competitors such as Apple and Microsoft have not brought their speedy JavaScript accelerators to the mobile platform (yet).

Today's JavaScript allows you to build desktop-like applications that run inside your web browser. Google's Wave solution is an excellent example of a massively complex application that is run using JavaScript.

JavaScript is the most popular development language in the world with millions of users. The technology is not too complex to learn; indeed if you have any experience with C#, Java, or ActionScript, then you will likely pick up JavaScript quickly.

JavaScript is so popular that it has its own standard. ECMA International is an industry association founded in 1961 and dedicated to the standardization of Information and Communication Technology (ICT) and Consumer Electronics (CE). The standardized version of JavaScript is managed by ECMA. The full standard name is ECMA-262, but is often referred to as EcmaScript. ECMA-262 as a standard is well-supported by all web browsers.

Geolocation on Your Phone

There is no doubt that the tech world is going mobile. Devices now need to know where they are geographically. In preparation for this, HTML5 includes support for geolocation. The iPhone and Android phones are already geolocation enabled, as shown in Figure 1.24.

The following example uses Google Map's service and the browser's geolocation API to tell you where you are located. The first step is to load the Map services.

```
<script src="http://maps.google.com/maps?file=api&am
p;v=2&amp;sensor=false&amp;key=ABQIAAAAiUzO1s6QWHuyzxx-
JVN7ABSUL8-Cfeleqd6F6deqY-Cw1iTxhxQkovZkaxsxgKCdn1OCYaq7Ub
z3SQ" type="text/javascript"></script>
```

The Google Map services are publically accessible. Now you need to start writing JavaScript. The first step is to define a series of variables that you can use in your code:

```
var map;
var mapCenter;
var geocoder;
var fakeLatitude;
var fakeLongitude;
```

With your JavaScript variables defined, you can create the first function that initializes the geolocation services in your web browser:

```
function initialize()
{
        if (navigator.geolocation)
        {
                navigator.geolocation.getCurrentPosition(
function (position) {
        mapServiceProvider(position.coords.latitude,position.
coords.longitude);
                },
        }
        else
        {
```

Figure 1.24 Google can use the GPS in your phone to detect where you are.

Use of Google Maps on a website requires a unique key. You can get all the information for getting a key at the web address code.google. com/apis/maps/.

```
          alert("I'm sorry, but Geolocation services are
not supported by your browser or you do not have a GPS
device in your computer. I will use a sample location to
produce the map instead.");
          fakeLatitude = 49.273677;
          fakeLongitude = -123.114420;
          mapServiceProvider(fakeLatitude,fakeLongitude);
          }
     }
```

The next function instructs the geolocation services to use the
Google Map service.

```
function mapServiceProvider(latitude,longitude)
{
          mapThisGoogle(latitude,longitude);
}
function mapThisGoogle(latitude,longitude)
{
       var mapCenter = new GLatLng(latitude,longitude);
       map = new GMap2(document.getElementById("map"));
       map.setCenter(mapCenter, 15);
       map.addOverlay(new GMarker(mapCenter));
       geocoder = new GClientGeocoder();
       geocoder.getLocations(latitude+','+longitude,
addAddressToMap);
     }
```

The final code completes the mapping:

```
function addAddressToMap(response)
{
       if (!response || response.Status.code != 200) {
              alert("Sorry, we were unable to geocode
that address");
       } else {
              place = response.Placemark[0];
              $('#address').html('Your address: '+place.
address);
       }
}
window.location.querystring = (function() {
  var collection = {};
  var querystring = window.location.search;
  if (!querystring) {
    return { toString: function() { return ""; } };
  }
  querystring = decodeURI(querystring.substring(1));
  var pairs = querystring.split("&");
  for (var i = 0; i < pairs.length; i++) {
    if (!pairs[i]) {
      continue;
    }
  var separatorPosition = pairs[i].indexOf("=");
```

```
    if (separatorPosition == -1) {
       collection[pairs[i]] = "";
    }
    else {
      collection[pairs[i].substring(0, separatorPosition)]
 = pairs[i].substr(separatorPosition + 1);
      }
    }
    collection.toString = function() {
      return "?" + querystring;
    };
    return collection;
})();
```

The final result is that you can use geolocation to determine where you are using just your web browser. This is very useful in mobile web browsers where you can link map services to geographically based tools.

Local Data Storage

Key to applications is the ability to store data. In the past you have been able to do this by using complex cookies or Ajax commands that leverage the ability to send data back to a database. The ability to store data locally in your web browser is dramatically improved with the implementation of LocalStorage.

LocalStorage is essentially the ability to have an SQL-like database running in your web browser. An example of LocalStorage being used is Google's version of Gmail for the iPhone/Android. Using LocalStorage, you can view and send e-mail with Gmail without having a web connection. The e-mail is resynchronized with the mail servers when a new network connection is established.

You access LocalStorage in your JavaScript by using the GlobalStorage object. The following example demonstrates LocalStorage being used.

The first step for the example in the previous image is to create an area where you can type some text. You will use standard form controls:

```
<textarea id="text" class="freetext">
</textarea> Item name <input id="item_name" type="text"
value="new item" />
```

An event will be added to the INPUT submit button to trigger the JavaScript to run:

```
<input onclick="writeLocal();" type="button" value="Save" />
```

The LocalStorage posts the data stored in the browser to the web page. An area with the ID "items" is defined.

```
<div id="items">
</div>
```

The first function run in your JavaScript is to define that the content on the page is to be associated with the website on which your page is being hosted:

```
function $(id) { return document.getElementById(id); }
var host = location.hostname;
var myLocalStorage = globalStorage[host];
```

The second function allows you to store data using the LocalStorage API:

```
function writeLocal() {
var data = $('text').value;
var itemName = $('item_name').value;
myLocalStorage.setItem(itemName, data);
updateItemsList();
}
```

As with any SQL database you need to be able to delete entries. The following function allows you to delete items using the removeItem property:

```
function deleteLocal(itemName) {
myLocalStorage.removeItem(itemName);
updateItemsList();
}
```

The following sample shows you the whole program with some simple CSS styling for presentation:

```
<html><head><title>HTML5 Web Storage / localStorage</
title></head>
<style>
.freetext {
        width: 100%;height: 40%;overflow: hidden;background:
#FFE;font-family: sans-serif;font-size: 14pt;-moz-border-radius:
10px;-webkit-border-radius: 10px;
  }
  li {
        padding: 4px;width: 400px;
  }
  input {
        margin: 2px;border-style: solid;-moz-border-radius:
10px;-webkit-border-radius: 10px;color: #666;padding: 2px;
  }
  body {
        font-family: "Lucida Sans", "Lucida Sans Regular",
"Lucida Grande", "Lucida Sans Unicode", Geneva, Verdana,
sans-serif;color: #FF0000;font-size: medium;
  }
  </style>
  <body><textarea id="text" class="freetext "></textarea>
Item name <input id="item_name" type="text" value="new item" />
<input onclick="writeLocal();" type="button" value="Save" />
<div id="items"></div>
  <script>
```

```
      function $(id) { return document.getElementById(id); }
      var host = location.hostname;
      var myLocalStorage = globalStorage[host];
      function writeLocal() {
       var data = $('text').value;
       var itemName = $('item_name').value;
       myLocalStorage.setItem(itemName, data);
       updateItemsList();
      }
      function deleteLocal(itemName) {
       myLocalStorage.removeItem(itemName);
       updateItemsList();
      }
      function readLocal(itemName) {
       $('item_name').value=itemName;
       $('text').value=myLocalStorage.getItem(itemName);
      }
      function updateItemsList() {
       var items = myLocalStorage.length
       // list items
       var s = '<h2>Items for '+host+'</h2>';
       s+= '<ul>';
       for (var i=0;i<items;i++) {
        var itemName = myLocalStorage.key(i);
        s+= '<li>'+
          '<div style="float:right;">'+
          '<input type="button" value="Load" onclick="readLocal
(\"+itemName+'\');"/'+'> '+
          '<input type="button" value="Delete" onclick="delete
Local(\"+itemName+'\');"/'+'> '+
          '</div>'+
          '<strong>'+itemName+'</strong>'+
          '</li>';
       }
       $('items').innerHTML = s+'</ul>';
      }
     window.onload = function() {
       updateItemsList();
       $('text').value=[
         'Quick and dirty Web Storage sample:','',
         '1) Write some text',
         '2) Give it some name',
         '3) Click Save button','',
         'Data is stored and retrieved using Web Storage (no
cookies and no server side).'].join('\n');
      }
     </script></body></html>
```

As you can see, the implementation of LocalStorage allows you
to store data without using cookies or server side databases.

Developing for Specific Mobile Browsers

The standards covered up to this point will work on all HTML5 web browsers, whether they are on your phone, laptop, TV, or tablet. Mobile phones have many additional features you can support. The goal of this section is to highlight popular features specific to different phones and to direct you to where you can get additional information.

Apple's Mobile Safari

At the time of this writing, there is a clear winner when it comes to advanced features in a mobile web browser: Apple. When iOS was first presented in January 2007, Steve Jobs went to great lengths to promise that Mobile Safari delivered "the whole web," not a broken presentation. Figure 1.25 is the first Mobile Safari logo.

On the whole, Apple has delivered on its promise. What you will find as you move through these articles, is that all the solutions will work on Apple's iOS. With that said, there is one major web feature supported by all mobile operating systems that Apple does not support: Adobe's Flash.

Figure 1.25 Mobile Safari logo.

Apple and Adobe are now enjoying an infamous power play over standards. Apple is pushing HTML5 and Adobe is pushing Flash. While the battle is interesting, Flash-enabled websites, such as game sites, do not work on the iPhone. Time will tell how this battle will resolve itself.

With that said, Apple's standards support in Mobile Safari is amazing. Mobile Safari has full support of SVG, embeddable TrueType fonts, HTML5 Video (using MPEG4), web sockets, and can even use hardware features such as Gyroscope and the Accelerometer through a DeviceOrientation API.

There are some HTML5 features still missing in Mobile Safari, most notably Web Workers. Web Workers are features in JavaScript that enable two or more scripts to run simultaneously, a critical feature for enterprise scale applications. Today, iOS does not allow for this.

You can find out more about specific iOS features in Mobile Safari at Apple's developer website, as shown in Figure 1.26 (*http://developer.apple.com/ios*).

Google's Android Browser

Google's Android browser, like Apple's, is built out from WebKit. A big challenge with Android, however, is fragmentation. Google provides the operating system as a free solution that can be adopted by any hardware company. The problem with this approach is that mobile phone companies such as Motorola, Samsung, and HTC can choose what they want to add and remove

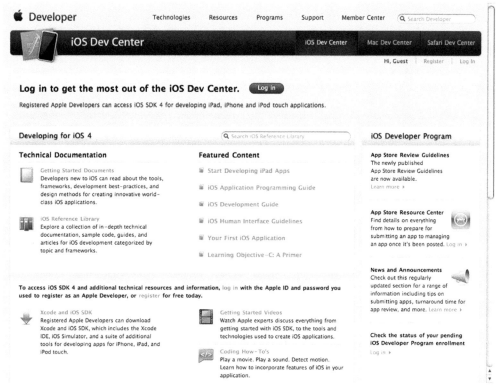

Figure 1.26 iOS developer site.

from the Android OS. For instance, some vendors include Google's V8 JavaScript accelerated engine but others do not. The result is that you do not have a consistent user experience. This does not mean you should not develop for Android; it just means you need to spend more time in your quality testing and controls.

Find out more about Android development at this site, as shown in Figure 1.27 (*http://developer.android.com/guide/*).

RIM's BlackBerry 6 and PlayBook

In many respects, RIM set the groundwork for today's smart phones with the BlackBerry phone. Within many corporations today, a BlackBerry phone is still very popular. But they are losing ground fast.

To compete against Apple and Google, RIM has done some solid soul searching and brought its core OS up to specification with competing technologies. The new BlackBerry 6 is sleek. And, guess what, the browser is based on WebKit. You know that means lots of HTML5.

Here are links to developer sections on BlackBerry 6 (Figure 1.28): *http://us.blackberry.com/apps-software/blackberry6/*.

Figure 1.27 Android developer site.

Figure 1.28 RIM's developer site.

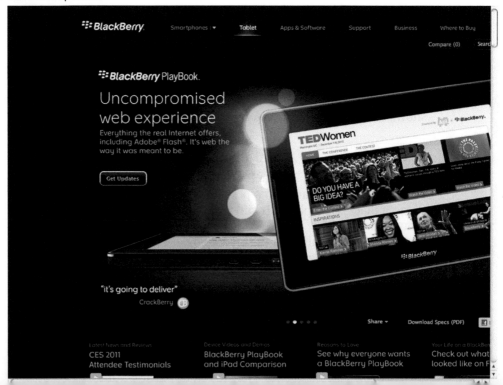

HP/Palm WebOS

HP acquired Palm and its WebOS platform in 2010. Since that time, HP has been very quiet about the acquisition. It is clear, however, that HP wants to enter the device market and that WebOS will be a competitive advantage for the company. The key to WebOS is that the whole OS is built using the web standards CSS, JavaScript, and HTML5. For more information check out *http://developer.palm.com/* (see Figure 1.29).

Developing Websites for the Rest

You may think that the term smart phone did not exist until the iPhone hit the scene. But the term itself has been around for many years, with many phones supporting web browsers since 2000. The problems they all share are poor support for standards and a terrible user experience. With that said, Nokia, the global leader in phone sales, has placed hundreds of millions of phones with web access into the hands of people around the world.

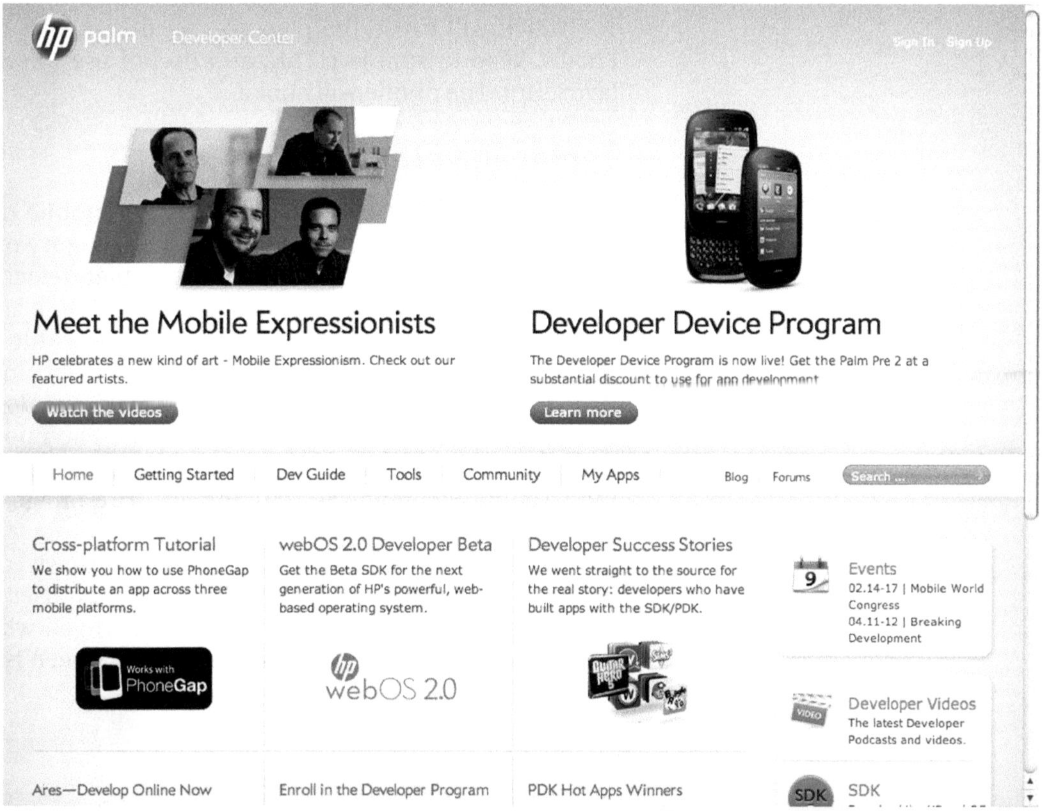

Figure 1.29 HP's WebOS developer site.

Nokia's MeeGo and Symbian

Nokia owns the mobile phone market. So why is it scared? The problem is that its two operating systems have not caught App fever and are not seen as platforms in the same light that Android and iOS are.

For this reason, Nokia is looking to change its core OS. Nokia has now agreed to support Windows Phone 7 OS.

Until then, you have MeeGo and Symbian. Both allow for apps to be downloaded, including web browsers. You can easily add Google Analytics to your website and see how many people are surfing to your website using Nokia phones. If your site does receive a lot of traffic from Nokia devices and you need to support them, keep this mantra close to your heart: keep it simple. Nokia phones are significantly underpowered compared to smart phones and even text-only web pages can take a long time to draw correctly on the screen.

Windows Phone 6.5 and Earlier

Windows Phone 6.5 was a big step forward when it came to the web browser even if those steps forward still placed it several steps behind Mobile Safari. Windows has improved a lot since the release of 6.5 with Windows Phone 7, but there are still a lot of 6.5 phones being used. When developing for these phones make sure you pay attention to the amount of content you place on a page. Too much will cause the page to take a very long time to load. Finally, keep to simple HTML and do not use too much CSS or JavaScript. The phone will choke.

Tablet Development

Much of this article places a focus on mobile development for smart phones. But, there is a second category of device that is gaining strong popularity—tablets. Tablet devices have been around for more than a decade, but it took Apple's iPad to reintroduce the category to the world. Apple was able to sell more than 17 million iPads from March through December of 2010. Following suit, Google introduced Android 3.0 Honeycomb as its competing tablet OS, RIM released the PlayBook, and HP is working on new tablets. The 2011 CES show presented more than 100 tablets. Figures 1.30 and 1.31 are images of the iPad and Honeycomb tablets, respectively.

Seems like we cannot get enough of them now!

As smart phones and laptops have different user experiences, so do tablets. Typically, tablet users are engaged with their content longer than smart phone users and the screen is much larger

Figure 1.30 Apple's iPad.   Figure 1.31 Google's Honeycomb tablet.

(though still smaller than a desktop). It still remains to be seen how to develop for tablets, but 2012 will be the year you start looking at tablets and considering how you need to ensure your website works for them as well as for smart phones and laptop computers.

Summary

The goal of this article was to introduce you to mobile web development. In many ways it is very similar to desktop website development—HTML5 is HTML5 no matter on which device you install it.

What is different is how you use and interface with the device. Smart phones are just very different devices to a laptop.

The next articles will introduce and review popular frameworks that allow you to quickly build out web sites that target smart phones. It is important to remember that each of these frameworks are built using the same HTML, CSS3, and JavaScript you have covered in detail in this article. What this means is that you can easily extend and enhance the frameworks you are about to use.

Let's roll up our sleeves and start creating web pages that target the device in your hand.

PROJECT: DEVELOPING YOUR FIRST MOBILE WEBSITE

In the previous article you were introduced to the new SECTION, ARTICLE, NAVIGATION, ASIDE, HEADER, and FOOTER elements in HTML5 that allow you to apply a more easily read structure to your website design. In this project you will be building an entire website that uses the new HTML5 blocking elements to illustrate how you can structure your code more effectively.

The website will consist of four pages:
- Home page
- Product page
- News page
- Contact us

Each of these pages demonstrates how you can use HTML5 in your website design. By the time you have completed this project you will able to apply blocking to your new design.

What You Will Need

To get started with this project you will need to download the files from *www.visualizetheweb.com*. The files for this project are contained in a ZIP file that you can extract on your desktop.

The project files include the following:
- CSS (Cascading Style Sheets)
- HTML

In many ways, this will be the easiest project for you to create. You are not using frameworks, just standard HTML5.

Setting Up Your Project

Each of the pages in the site will highlight specific elements used in HTML5. To make things easy for you let's set up one page that you can reuse as a template for the other pages in the project

Figure P1.1 HTML5 and CSS3 are used to construct the document.

website. It is easier to manage your website when the HTML code is consistent on each page. Finding and replacing sections becomes a matter of cut and paste. For this project, the default home page contains all the elements and structure you will need for the entire site. The home page, as shown in Figure P1.1, will be used as the template.

Before you start coding your HTML let's take some time to explore how the default home page is structured. You will want to use a tool that allows you to easily draw blocks on the page to visually show where you will place the content.

There are four basic sections to each web page. HTML5 allows you to block out the following sections:
- Header
- Section
- Navigation
- Footer

The basic structure for the page looks like this in HTML5:

```
<!DOCTYPE html>
<head>
<meta content="en-us" http-equiv="Content-Language" />
<meta content="text/html; charset=utf-8" http-
equiv="Content-Type" />
<link href="style.css" rel="stylesheet" type="text/css" />
<title>Company Home Page</title>
</head>
<body>
<header >      </header>
<navigation>  </navigation>
<section>     </section>
<footer>      </footer>
</body>
</html>
```

The default page opens with the HTML5 DOCTYPE that declares that the page supports HTML5. The rest of the HTML code within the HEAD element has not changed in HTML5. It is not until you start creating the content in the main page that you will see the new HTML5 elements.

The new blocking elements in HTML5 describe accurately where the content goes. In HTML4 and XHTML you can only achieve this same type of layout using DIV elements that are difficult to manage. It is easier to understand what each section is attempting to achieve when you name the elements HEADER, FOOTER, SECTION, and NAVIGATION.

Now that you have your basic page structure, you can start filling in each section with content.

Customizing the HEADER Element

The HEADER element in the project example contains only one key part: a search engine. To add a Google Search engine insert the following code:

```
<header id="header" class="headerStyle" >
        <form method="get" action="http://www.google.
com/search">
        <input type="text" name="q" size="15"
maxlength="255" value="" placeholder="Search" />
        <input type="submit" value="GO" />
        <input type="hidden" name="sitesearch" value=
"www.focalpress.com" />
        </form>
</header>
```

The HEADER element has two additional attributes: ID and Class. The ID is a value that, if you insert JavaScript into the page, you can use to identify the HEADER element on the page. The Class attribute "headerStyle" links to a style defined in the CSS file. The headerStyle describes the placement and visual presentation of the HEADER element on the screen.

Inside the HEADER element is the FORM element. The FORM element takes any content entered in the INPUT element and sends it to Google.

The first INPUT element is using a new HTML5 Form attribute. The Placeholder attribute allows you to add ghosted text into the input form that disappears when you start typing your own content.

A final hidden INPUT element forces the search engine results to search only www.focalpress.com.

Customizing the Main SECTION Element

The center area of the web page is reserved for the main content. The HTML for this section can be described as easily as this:

```
<section> </section>
```

Typically you will find that the main section of any web page will contain more content. The template page is set up with two areas for additional content within the SECTION element.

```
<section>
<div id="section_articleOneIdentifier" style="position:
absolute; left: 355px; top: 105px; width: 1px; height:
60px; z-index: 3">
        <hr class="style2" style="height: 60px; width:
1px" /></div>
```

```
<article id="article_one" style="position: absolute;
left: 420px; top: 100px; width: 315px; height: 195px;
z-index: 2">
        <h1>Header 1</h1>
        <p>Add Content here</p></article>
    <div id="section_articleTwoIdentifier" style="position:
absolute; left: 355px; top: 355px; width: 1px; height:
60px; z-index: 3">
        <hr class="style2" style="height: 60px; width:
1px" /></div>
    <article id="article_two" style="position: absolute;
left: 420px; top: 350px; width: 315px; height: 195px;
z-index: 2">
        <h1>Header 2</h1>
        <p>Add Content here</p>
</article>
<hr class="HRstyle" style="position: absolute; left:
420px; top: 320px; width: 315px; height: 2px; z-index: 3" />
</section>
```

Two ARTICLE elements are placed within the SECTION element. The ID for both ARTICLE elements is unique to allow you to easily identify which element is which. Instead of linking to an external CSS class a Style attribute is used for both ARTICLE elements. The Style attribute is using CSS but it is localized to that single element and is not shared with other elements.

Each ARTICLE element also contains an H1 element and P elements. The H1 element is a header used to lead in each article title. The P element is a paragraph element for content. Placeholder text is added to H1 and P tags so you can see where the content is when you view the page in an HTML5-compliant web browser.

The final HR (horizontal rule) element is a visual separator between the two ARTICLE elements.

Customizing the FOOTER Element

The final element to modify is the FOOTER element. The following code describes the FOOTER element:

```
<footer id="footer" class="footerStyle">
        <hr class="HRstyle" />
        <p class="Copyright">Copyright © 2011 Focal Press</p>
</footer>
```

Typically, the FOOTER element does not contain much information. An HR element is used to visually separate the FOOTER element from the content on the page. Below the HR element is a P element that contains copyright information. Again, CSS is used to style and position the elements on the screen.

At this point you can take your HTML and save it. Name your file template.html.

The layout is constructed with HTML content, with the visual elements controlled with CSS. The final project will show all the content in the correct placement on the screen.

Creating the Home Page for the Website

In many ways, the home page for your website is the easiest to create. You have already done all the heavy lifting creating the template for the website. For the home page, all you have to do is switch out the content you entered as placeholder text with the text you want to have displayed on your home page.

Open the template.html file and save the file as default.html. This will be your new home page file.

Each of the ARTICLE elements in the main SECTION element will be modified to reflect new content. Using a unique ID for each ARTICLE makes it easier to work with each section. Find the ARTICLE with the ID article_one and replace the HTML code with the following:

```
<article id="article_one" style="position: absolute;
left: 420px; top: 100px; width: 315px; height: 195px;
z-index: 2">
   <p id="section_articleTwoIdentifier" style="position:
absolute; left: 355px; top: 105px; width: 1px; height:
60px; z-index: 3">
   <hr class="style2" style="height: 60px; width: 1px" />
</p>
   <h1>Welcome to our Site</h1>
   <strong>Cras ut justo eu arcu</strong> varius viverra
in a enim. Nulla varius pharetra luctus. Ut scelerisque
consequat velit at accumsan. <br /><br />
   <strong>Sed euismod eros</strong> ut massa commodo
egestas. Ut fringilla tincidunt ligula quis blandit. In et
vestibulum orci. <br /><br />
   <strong>Donec et metus sed</strong> purus ultrices
interdum vel non purus. Nulla nisi velit, vulputate nec
sodales vitae, dignissim quis odio. Praesent malesuada
pulvinar leo, vel ultricies metus eleifend at.</article>
```

This code keeps the content within the ARTICLE element. A search engine, such as Google.com or Bing.com, can now accurately identify this content as informational and pertinent to the page. Identifying pertinent information is the goal of a search engine and will help in allowing this page to appear higher in the results page for Google or Bing.

The second ARTICLE element contains the following HTML code:

```
<article id="article_two" style="position: absolute;
left: 420px; top: 350px; width: 315px; height: 195px;
z-index: 2">
    <p id="section_articleOneIdentifier" style="position:
absolute; left: 355px; top: 355px; width: 1px; height:
60px; z-index: 3">
    <hr class="style2" style="height: 60px; width: 1px" />
</p>
    <h1>What we do</h1>
    <p>Nullam tincidunt pulvinar ornare.</p>
    <p><strong>Our Products</strong> </p>
    <p>Phasellus dictum elementum erat, rutrum pellentesque
tellus imperdiet ac. Sed quis porttitor eros. </p>
    <p><strong>Our Services</strong></p>
    <p>Etiam gravida dui a purus sollicitudin tempus
blandit sem pulvinar.</p>
    </article>
```

The second ARTICLE uses different HTML to format the text. The new HTML elements do not restrict you from using additional elements within them, giving you maximum creative freedom to code a page the way you want it coded.

This is it. Save the page and view it through your favorite HTML5-compliant web browser.

Figure P1.2 The ASIDE HTML5 element is fully supported in most smart phones.

Adding a News Page That Uses the TIME and ASIDE Elements

The next page to create is the news page. The news page uses two elements that help provide additional information about both content and structure content on the screen. Figure P1.2 shows you what the page looks like.

Let's start by adding the sidebar shown on the screen. Open the template.html file and save it at news.html.

The sidebar is created using the ASIDE element. As with other blocking elements, the goal of the ASIDE is to help you structure your content. In this example, you go one step further and format the position and presentation of the aside using CSS.

The following HTML code creates the ASIDE:

```
<aside id="aside" style="position: absolute; left:
740px; top: 200px; width: 150px; height: 190px; z-index:
6; background-color: #808080; color: #FFFFFF;-moz-border-
radius: 10px;-webkit-border-radius: 10px;padding: 5px;">
    </aside>
```

The Style attribute defines the position, background color, and border radius so you can see ASIDE on the page. Place the ASIDE element within the SECTION element. The following HTML can be added within the ASIDE element tags. This is the content for the ASIDE:

```
    For additional information on press releases please
contact:<br /><br />
    Production Information<br />
    John Marshall<br />
    <a href="mailto:jmarshall@email.com">jmarshall@email.
com</a><br /><br />
    Corporate Information<br />
    Jenny Smythe<br />
    <a href="mailto:jsmythe@email.com">jsmythe@email.com</a>
<br /><br />
    Phone Calls:<br />
    (920) 555-1212<br />
```

Both ARTICLE elements contain information that is newsworthy. A date for each news article specifies the publication date. Using the TIME element you can highlight the time content for each article on the page.

Following is the title and date for the first article:

```
    <h1>The news is hot!</h1>
    <p><time>April 1, 2010</time></p>
```

In this instance, the TIME element captures the information between the two tags and identifies it as a date. The second news headline uses the Datetime attribute to be more specific with the date:

```
    <h1>What we do</h1>
    <p><time datetime="2010-03-15T10:32:17">March 15,
2010</time></p>
```

Here the text between the TIME elements states March 15, 2010. The Datetime attribute allows additional information to be added. In this case, the Datetime attribute adds a time stamp to the date, explaining that the article was published as 10:32 AM and 17 seconds.

Creating a Contact Us Page That Uses the New Form Input Attributes

Earlier in this chapter you built a search engine form that sends requests to Google. The Contact Us form (Figure P1.3) builds on the fundamentals introduced with the Google Search form and introduces you to more complex ways in which you can display data.

Figure P1.3 Forms work correctly on any modern mobile device.

The form automatically places the focus of the cursor into the First Name field (this field is required). The Middle Name field has been disabled, preventing a user from entering data into it. The Age field is a numeric scroll that allows you to choose an age from 18 to 100. The Email field has a visual cue to tell you that you must enter a valid e-mail address. The How Did You Hear about Us? field is a drop-down that allows you to choose from several options. The When Would You Like Us to Contact You? field is a selectable date tool. The final field, How Many of Our Products Do You Own?, is a slider, allowing you to choose from 0 to 10.

The new attributes for the INPUT element enable you to accomplish complex design without having to develop complex scripting solutions or leverage nonstandard technologies such as Adobe Flash or Microsoft Silverlight.

What has not changed in HTML5 forms is the way you send data using CGI or Server Side technologies such as PHP, ASP.NET, ColdFusion, or JSP. You can use any CGI solution to transmit data captured in a web form. HTML5 only gives you more options to capture the data—once you have the data, it is still data.

To create the Contact Us form you will need to take a copy of the template.html file and save it as contactus.html. Open the contactus.html file in your favorite text editor. The form will be added to the main SECTION block of the page.

The first elements to add are the opening and closing FORM elements.

```
<h1>Contact Us</h1>
<p>For more information, contact us:</p>
<form method="POST" action="http://fp1.formmail.com/
cgi-bin/fm192">
</form>
```

In this code you have a title and brief sentence introducing the form. The FORM element uses the POST method to submit the contents of the form. In this example I am using the free FormMail service to submit the contents of the form. You can use this for your forms, too. The action=http://fp1.formmail.com/cgi-bin/fm192 submits the data from the form to a free CGI Perl script.

INPUT form elements are placed in-between the opening and closing FORM element. The following three INPUT elements are hidden. The role of these elements is to pass data to the CGI Perl script, letting it know that the form is valid and where to send the results when someone has completed the form.

```
<input type="hidden" name="_pid" value="119137">
<input type="hidden" name="_fid" value="FNNZXGED">
<input type="hidden" name="recipient"
value="matthewadavid@gmail.com">
```

Here you can swap the recipient e-mail with your own.

The visual elements of the form use the LABEL and INPUT elements to present themselves on the page. The LABEL element identifies the text as a label and is typically used with forms. As with the TIME, MARK, and METER elements, the LABEL element is a new blocking HTML5 feature. Each form INPUT element has a preceding LABEL describing the element. The LABEL element does not have any additional attributes. The following is the LABEL for the first field in the form:

```
<label>First Name: </label><br />
```

A BR element is used to force a single line break after the LABEL element.

The following HTML code allows you to force the cursor to start in this field by adding the Autofocus attribute. The Required attribute also prevents the form from being submitted until a value has been entered into the First Name field.

```
<label>First Name: </label><br /><input name=
"FirstName" type="text" autofocus required> <br /><br />
```

The Middle Name INPUT field has been visually disabled. You can use the disable feature to lock and unlock fields dynamically using JavaScript.

```
<label>Middle Name: </label><br /><input name="MiddleName"
type="text" disabled>
```

The Last Name field is also a required field using the Required attribute.

```
<label>Last Name: </label><br /><input name="LastName"
type="text" maxlength="25" required> <br /><br />
```

The Age field is a numeric stepper tool that allows you to scroll through a specific range of numbers. In this case, you can choose a number from 18 to 100.

The visual effect of the numeric stepper is created through setting the attribute settings of type, min, and max. Here is the HTML code for the Age field:

```
<label>Age: </label><br /><input name="age"
type="number" min="18" max="100"><br /><br />
```

The Type attribute identifies the INPUT element as a numeric stepper. Placing a min and max value forces the element to be restricted between those two numbers.

The Email field uses the INPUT type attribute Email to force the visual e-mail icon to appear at the beginning of the field.

The code to add these Email and Required visual cues is:

```
<label>Email: </label><br /><input name="email"
type="email" required><br /><br />
```

As you can see, all you need to do is identify the INPUT as a type=email and insert the Required attribute.

The most complex INPUT element allows you to choose from three items in a drop-down. The drop-down is accomplished by creating a datalist and linking it to an INPUT element. The following creates the list. The key attribute is the ID in the first line. The ID in the datalist can be linked to other elements on the page.

```
<datalist id="mylist">
<option label="google" value="http://google.com">
<option label="yahoo" value="http://yahoo.com">
<option label="Bing" value="http://bing.com">
</datalist>
```

An INPUT element can now be linked to the datalist using the following code:

```
<label>How did you hear about us?: </label><br /><input
name="HowDidYouHear" type="uri" list="mylist"><br /><br />
```

The INPUT element uses the List attribute to link the ID of the datalist. The datalist values are now injected into the INPUT element.

Frequently you will see a tool used on web pages that enables you to select a date. With HTML5 you can add a date picker simply by identifying the INPUT element as the type "date." The following code is all you need to add:

```
<label>When would you like us to contact you?: </label><br />
<input name="ContactDate" type="date"><br /><br />
```

Changing the Type attribute to "date" adds a sophisticated date picker.

Before selecting the Submit button, you can answer the last question in the form by sliding a scrub head to choose a number from 0 to 10. The value you select appears as a number to the right of the slider.

Using the slider and displaying the value you select uses both a new Type attribute in the INPUT field and the new OUTPUT field. The slider uses the new Range type attribute. As with the Number type attribute, the Range attribute also supports minimum (min) and maximum (max) values. You can also force the slider to start at a specific number using the Value attribute. The following code defines the INPUT as a Range with the min set at 0, the max set at 10, and the Value set at 5, positioning the slider in the center.

```
<label>How many of our products do you own?: </label><br />
<input id="slider" name="sliderValue" type="range" min="1"
max="10" value="5"> </input>
```

You will also see in this code that the ID of the INPUT element is "sliderValue." The OUTPUT element can link to the ID and post the value onto the web page. The following code shows you how to do this.

```
<output name="NumberOfProducts" value="5" onforminput=
"value=sliderValue.value" >5</output><br /><br />
```

The final element to add to the FORM is the BUTTON element. Here is the code:

```
<button type=submit>Submit</button>
```

As you can see, nothing special is applied to the BUTTON element. Sorry, just plain old-fashioned HTML here, folks.

Summary

The project covered in this chapter illustrates how you can successfully use the HTML5 blocking elements to more effectively manage your HTML code within your mobile projects. Without having to resort to complex and confusing HTML TABLES or DIV elements, the new HEADER, SECTION, ARTICLE, ASIDE, NAVIGATION, and FOOTER elements logically places content on the screen.

The new form attributes allow you to add a slew of new visual tools to capture data. The new INPUT types are both sophisticated and simple to insert. You no longer need to work with complex Ajax libraries to add a date picker. All you need to do is modify an INPUT type.

The role of these new elements is to enable you to more easily control the content as it is presented in HTML. How that data is presented is controlled using CSS.

DEVELOPING WEBSITES WITH jQUERY MOBILE

One of the most popular frameworks used to build out complex web pages is jQuery, an Open Source solution managed by community volunteers. This article is going to take a deep dive in jQuery for mobile development. You will use the specialized jQuery Mobile framework and jQuery itself to add complexity and riches to your pages.

Progressive Enhancement

You probably have one in your pocket, or you may be talking to it, or you may be playing games on it—it's a smart phone. The category of smart phone seems to be quite broad—is it an Android phone, Apple iOS device, WebOS, or something else?

It is a royal pain in the neck to develop websites optimized for a mobile device when there are literally so many different types out there. To give you a taste, here is a list of just some mobile devices:

- Apple iPhone/iPod Touch
- Google Android
- RIM BlackBerry/PlayBook OS
- Nokia Symbian (retired, but still with over 1 billion users worldwide)
- HP/Palm WebOS
- Microsoft Windows Phone Series

This list covers just the names of the operating systems and does not even start to break down the different browser versions.

The challenge you have with such a vast number of different systems is fragmented support for standards. For instance, Apple's latest iPhone has amazing support for HTML5, whereas

Symbian and the Microsoft Windows Phone Series have little to none. To battle this, jQuery employs a philosophy called progressive enhancement. Figure 2.1 is an image showing jQuery running on four different mobile operating systems.

At its roots, progressive enhancement means this: If you have the latest web browser then you will get all the bells and whistles; if you have an older browser then the page will still render and you will still have access to the content.

The goal is to allow you as a developer and designer to add complex features such as 3D page transitions found in iOS, but still have the page load and function on devices that are several years old.

The bottom line is that progressive enhancement is a model that allows your content to work at any level of browser (desktop, mobile, tablet, or TV).

Figure 2.1 Each of these devices run jQuery Mobile—all are different operating systems and web browsers.

What Is jQuery?

When you work in jQuery you tend to forget some of the obvious questions such as: What is jQuery? The focus of this section is to explain what jQuery is and, when your boss asks, why it's important to your work.

jQuery was released in January 2006 by John Resig as an Open Source JavaScript library to make it easier to add complex interactivity to your web applications using JavaScript, but with the promise of working across all popular web browsers. This is no mean feat, since jQuery has to support many different variations of browsers (IE6–9, Firefox 1–4, Safari, Chrome, Opera, to name just a handful). Figure 2.2 shows jQuery's website.

For the most part, jQuery has stuck true to its roots and has garnered a huge following of developers. It is estimated that more than 3000 of the top 10,000 popular sites use jQuery, making it

Figure 2.2 You can download jQuery at *www.jquery.com*.

the most popular JavaScript library being used. Part of the reason jQuery is so popular is due to how easy it is to add to your web pages. You can be up and running in jQuery by adding one single line of code in your web page:

```
<script type="text/javascript"
  src=" http://ajax.googleapis.com/ajax/libs/jquery/1.5/
jquery.min.js"> </script>
```

This path points directly to the Google-hosted version of jQuery. Figure 2.3 shows jQuery located inside of the HTML of a web page.

Amazingly, this whole JavaScript library is only 24 Kb when you use the compressed "min" version. So, what do you get for this? Let me point you to the jQuery API for the details (*http:// api.jquery.com/*), but I will give you a summary here (see also Figure 2.4):

- Ajax call tools (for real asynchronous control of your XML)
- CSS control through the DOM
- Data control

Figure 2.3 You need only one line to reference jQuery.

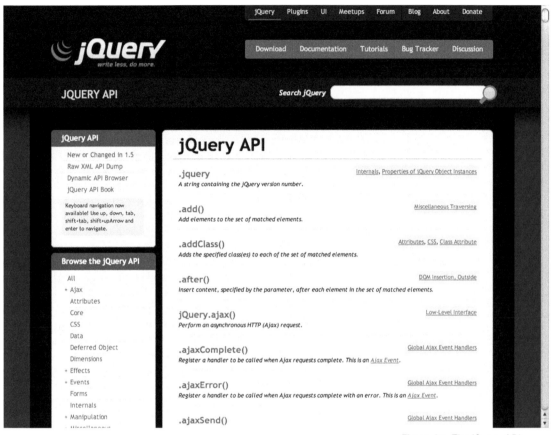

Figure 2.4 The jQuery API.

- Visual effects
- Consistent event actions
- DOM manipulation
- Properties
- Selectors
- Utilities

In other words, you get a lot in a very small package.

John Resig has a great tutorial called "How jQuery Works" (*http://docs.jquery.com/How_jQuery_Works*) that you can read on the jQuery website.

Here is an example of writing your own JavaScript with the jQuery library. I am using John's example here (thanks, John, if you are reading):

```
$(document).ready(function(){
  $("a").click(function(event){
    alert("jQuery ROCKS!");
  });
});
```

So, what's going on here? The first declaration is the $ sign. What the heck is up with the $ sign? Well, the $ sign is a keyword function that references the main jQuery Object in the JS library. So, instead of writing out *jQuery ("a").click(function(event))* you can use the $. Believe you me, this will save your tired digits a lot of time from tapping on the keyboard.

The first parenthesis is (document).ready, which is an event in jQuery that checks that all of the web page and images have downloaded before the code executes.

The second line adds a function to any "A", ANCHOR element you may have on your web page. When the ANCHOR is selected an alert pops up (see line 3).

To test this out, add the following HTML to the body of your code:

```
<a href="http://www.focalpress.com">Click me</a>
```

Test the effect in *any* web browser and the alert will work the same.

You might be thinking, "you told me that jQuery would reduce the amount of JavaScript that I am writing, but you have me writing code! What gives?" You are writing code, but jQuery allows you to write much less code.

There is also another way to get jQuery to do more for you: it's called plug-ins.

A plug-in references the main jQuery library in a second JS file to give you additional functionality such as adding form validation, a chart tool, or a sortable table. A current list of plug-ins is available at *http://plugins.jquery.com/*, as shown in Figure 2.5. Currently, there are over 1000 plug-ins for jQuery.

You will see that there are two groups of plug-ins: core plug-ins and community plug-ins. The core plug-ins are extensions to jQuery that are considered part of the core project. The most popular core plug-in is jQuery UI, a user interface plug-in that includes several cool tools such as tabs, accordion, and drag-n-drop; Microsoft has recently contributed Templates, Data Link, and Globalization as additional core plug-ins.

Finally, jQuery gives you an easy way to structure your code. It is clean, organized, and optimized. In fact, it fits in perfectly with any MVC project you are developing (MVC stands for Model View Controller, a pattern for keeping the domain logic and user interface elements separated) with ASP.NET, PHP, or the many languages that support MVC.

Figure 2.5 The jQuery plug-ins library.

Going beyond the Core of jQuery

At one time, when you said jQuery it was clear you were referring to the core JavaScript library. Today? Not so much. As the web and access to the web is changing, so is jQuery. Today there several pieces that makes the jQuery toolset. They are:

- jQuery Core (*www.jquery.com*)
- jQuery UI (*www.jqueryui.com*)
- jQuery Mobile (*www.jquerymobile.com*)
- jQuery Plug-ins (*plugins.jquery.com*)

At the center of your jQuery world is the core library, a 26 Kb minified Gzip slice of goodness. The core library has matured dramatically over the last five or so years to meet the jQuery Groups' goals of "write less, do more" mantra. Meeting this goal requires a dedicated core team with a focus on quality.

All the other parts of jQuery can be considered plug-ins, building out from the core library. With that said, some plug-ins are so

Figure 2.6 The jQuery UI website.

huge that they do deserve their own section. A great example of a set of plug-ins that is now part of the top-tier is jQuery UI, as shown in Figure 2.6. The jQuery user interface library allows you to easily add to your site controls such as sliders, accordions, and datapickers. In addition, jQuery UI enables you to apply a consistent set of styles to your site using ThemeRoller, a web-based CSS style engine.

The last two years have seen an explosion of mobile tools. To meet this demand comes the newest part of the jQuery family: jQuery Mobile, as shown in Figure 2.7. The goal of jQuery Mobile is to make it easier to build consistent mobile websites for a growing group of devices. This is not an easy goal when you consider how different iPhones, iPads, BlackBerry PlayBooks, and Android phones can all present the web. Expect jQuery Mobile to iterate and grow dramatically over the next year.

The final piece that makes up the jQuery framework is the extensible plug-in architecture built into jQuery that allows for hundreds of developers to extend the Core UI with specialized plug-ins. There are some plug-ins, such as Microsoft's Templates plug-in, that are becoming top-tier plug-ins along with jQuery UI

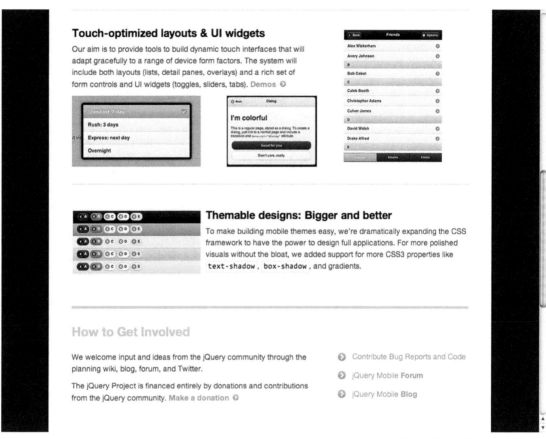

Figure 2.7 The jQuery mobile site.

and jQuery Mobile libraries. Other plug-ins have a narrow focus to meet a specific need such as the following:

- jQTouch: The mother of mobile environments. You have to check out this open source solution for any mobile website you need to develop (*www.jqtouch.com*), as shown in Figure 2.8.
- Hi-res images for retina displays: Apple made a big splash about the "retina display" for the iPhone 4 supporting a massive 300+ ppi resolution images, but other phones running Android have been doing this for a while. This means you will want to switch out the dusty low-res images we use for computers (c'mon, people, who wants to see a 96 ppi image, it's like watching regular TV after you have had HD!) for hi-res alternatives. Check out Troy Mcilvena's jQuery Retina Display plug-in (*http://troymcilvena.com/post/998277515/jquery-retina*). All your images will swap out low-res with hi-res. Sweet!
- jQuery iPhone plug-in: This project has not been updated for a while, but it might give you some extras (*http://plugins.jquery. com/project/iphone*).

Figure 2.8 jQTouch website.

- jQuery itself is going mobile: The new goal for jQuery is to run on all sorts of devices, not just desktops. Check out *http://jquerymobile.com/* for more details.

There are other plug-ins you can use, but these are a collection I have used that I have really liked. Some I have used a lot (such as jQTouch) and some are brand new.

Developing Websites Using jQuery Mobile

Developing mobile websites is no longer a wish list item for the web design team: it's a reality. The adoption of mobile devices is growing at a rapid pace. Within the next two years you may well see more people coming to your website on a phone or tablet instead of using a traditional computer.

Over the last 18 months a small collection of frameworks that specifically target mobile devices have sprung up, the most recent being jQuery Mobile. You can find out more information on jQuery Mobile at its website: *http://jquerymobile.com/*.

There are two paths you can take in developing a mobile framework: create a standalone framework that targets mobile browsers or build on top of an existing framework. The folks over at jQuery decided to do both. The current release of jQuery Mobile extends the Core jQuery framework with some specific mobile features and augments the core with a second library, jQuery Mobile. In essence, jQuery Mobile is a super plug-in for jQuery Core (much in the same way that jQuery UI and Templates are big plug-ins for jQuery Core).

In this section you are going to learn how you can implement jQuery Mobile into your websites.

The goal of jQuery Mobile is to allow the framework to run on as many mobile devices as possible. In the United States the primary focus is on iOS and Android smart phones. However, outside of the United States, other carriers, such as Nokia, are dominant. To this end, jQuery Mobile will work on a broad set of devices. At the launch of jQuery Mobile, in September 2010, John Resig, the author of jQuery, revealed a chart that listed the most popular mobile operating systems (*http://jquerymobile.com/gbs/*), as shown in Figure 2.9.

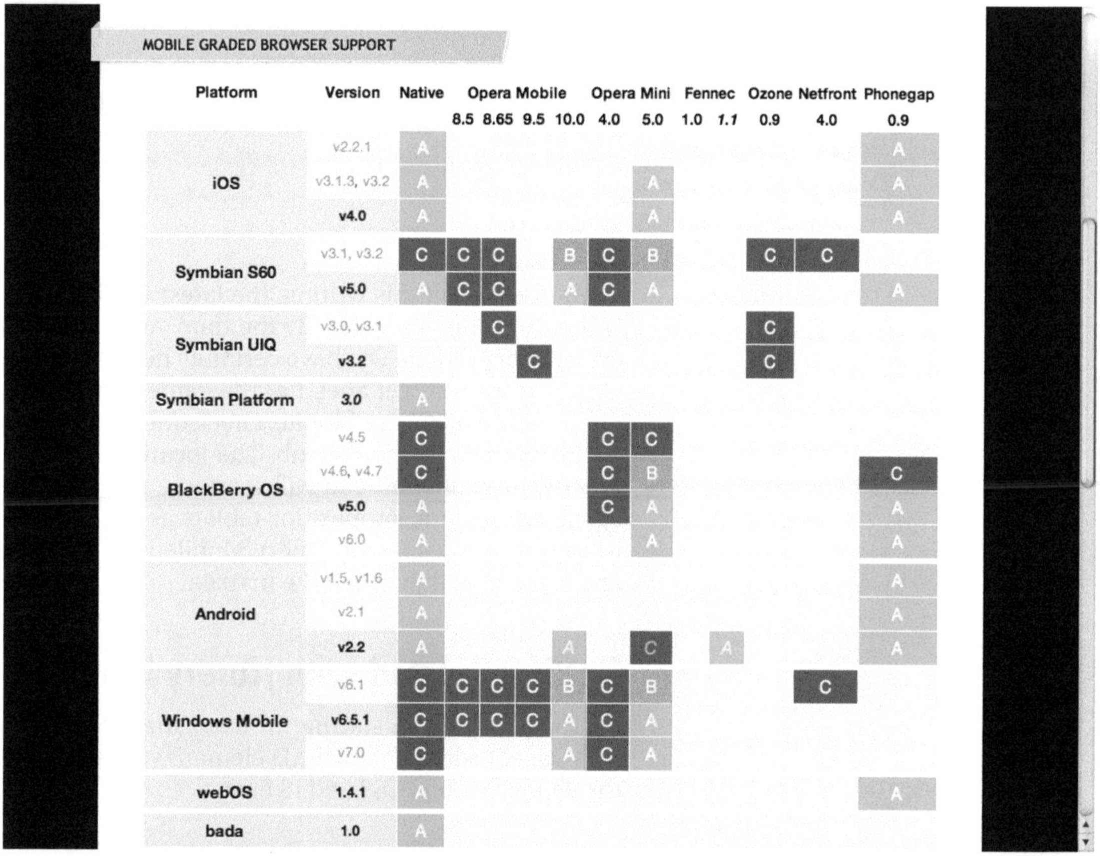

Figure 2.9 Grade for mobile browsers.

MOBILE GRADED BROWSER SUPPORT

Platform	Version	Native	Opera Mobile 8.5	Opera Mobile 8.65	Opera Mobile 9.5	Opera Mobile 10.0	Opera Mini 4.0	Opera Mini 5.0	Fennec 1.0	Fennec 1.1	Ozone 0.9	Netfront 4.0	Phonegap 0.9
iOS	v2.2.1	A											A
	v3.1.3, v3.2	A						A					A
	v4.0	A						A					A
Symbian S60	v3.1, v3.2	C	C	C			B	C	B		C	C	
	v5.0	A	C	C			A	C	A				A
Symbian UIQ	v3.0, v3.1				C						C		
	v3.2					C					C		
Symbian Platform	3.0	A											
BlackBerry OS	v4.5	C					C	C					
	v4.6, v4.7	C						C	B				C
	v5.0	A						C	A				A
	v6.0	A							A				A
Android	v1.5, v1.6	A											A
	v2.1	A											A
	v2.2	A						A	C	A			A
Windows Mobile	v6.1	C	C	C	C		B	C	B		C		
	v6.5.1	C	C	C	C		A	C	A				
	v7.0	C					A	C	A				
webOS	1.4.1	A											A
bada	1.0	A											

For each system he assigned an A, B, or C, the letters determining if the importance of supporting the OS was high (A), medium (B), or low (C). The following are determined to be of high importance (A) for support within jQuery Mobile:

- iOS (for iPhones, iPod Touch, and iPads)
- Symbian S60
- Symbian Platform
- BlackBerry OS 5 and 6
- Android
- WebOS
- bada
- MeeGo

Devices at the bottom of the scale include the following:

- Windows Mobile
- Maemo

As an indication of how rapidly the mobile world is changing, this whole matrix will likely now be redrawn due to one radical change: Nokia is killing the Symbian platform and replacing it with Windows Mobile Phone 7. In one move, Windows Mobile Phone 7 has gone from being irrelevant to immediately relevant. In addition, Nokia is also dropping MeeGo, and bada remains relevant only to Samsung phones (*Note:* Samsung is moving aggressively to adopt Android globally, replacing its own aging bada operating system). The new A-list should now read:

- iOS
- BlackBerry 6
- Android
- WebOS
- Windows Mobile

At the time of this writing, the latest version of jQuery Mobile is the third Alpha release. By the time you are reading this, however, jQuery Mobile will have certainly hit 1.0.

If you want to get ahead of the game and see what is coming to the future of jQuery Mobile, check out the Experiments section of the source code in GitHub. The location is *https://github.com/jquery/jquery-mobile.* You will see some very interesting technologies that include support for tablets as well as smart phones. It is clear that the goal for jQuery Mobile is to include new devices and screens as they reach the market.

Getting Started with jQuery Mobile

The first step in starting to use jQuery Mobile is to set up a web page. Inside of the HEAD element you will want to reference the jQuery Mobile CSS and JS files:

```
<link rel="stylesheet" href=" http://code.jquery.com/
mobile/1.0a3/jquery.mobile-1.0a3.min.css" />
   <script src=" http://code.jquery.com/jquery-1.5.min.
js"> </script>
   <script src=" http://code.jquery.com/mobile/1.0a3/
jquery.mobile-1.0a3.min.js"> </script>
```

As you can see from the script source files, jQuery Mobile is extending the core jQuery library. For you resource watchers out there, the current minified file size for jQuery Mobile is 12 Kb.

The source references in the JavaScript above point to the live CDN (Content Delivery Network) versions hosted on the jQuery servers. The CSS link also contains all the graphic files you need.

If you want to download and host the files locally you will need to go to the following web address, also shown in Figure 2.10: *http://code.jquery.com/mobile/1.0a3/jquery.mobile-1.0a3.zip.*

Figure 2.10 Where to get jQuery Mobile.

Download

We provide CDN-hosted versions of jQuery Mobile for you to include into your site. These are already minified and compressed – and host the image files as well. It'll likely be the fastest way to include jQuery Mobile in your site.

CDN-Hosted JavaScript:

- Uncompressed: jquery-mobile-1.0a3.js (130KB, useful for debugging)
- Minified and Gzipped: jquery-mobile-1.0a3.min.js (17KB, ready to deploy)

CDN-Hosted CSS:

- Uncompressed: jquery-mobile-1.0a3.css (53KB, useful for debugging)
- Minified and Gzipped: jquery-mobile-1.0a3.min.css (7KB, ready to deploy)

Copy-and-Paste Snippet:

```
<link rel="stylesheet" href="http://code.jquery.com/mobile/1.0a3/jquery.mobile-1.0a3.min.css" />
<script src="http://code.jquery.com/jquery-1.5.min.js"></script>
<script src="http://code.jquery.com/mobile/1.0a3/jquery.mobile-1.0a3.min.js"></script>
```

More details on how this works can be found in the page and layout documentation.

If you want to host the files yourself you can download a zip of all the files:

ZIP File:

- Zip File: jquery-mobile-1.0a3.zip (JavaScript, CSS, and images)

Testing

Figure 2.11 The basic boilerplate demo of jQuery Mobile running on an iPhone.

Download and expand the ZIP file. Within the file you will find compressed and uncompressed versions of the CSS and JavaScript files along with a subfolder containing 10 images used by the CSS document.

There are three basic areas of content on your web page that you will need to use when building your first jQuery Mobile site. The following is a boilerplate template jQuery provides, shown on an iPhone in Figure 2.11:

```
<!DOCTYPE html>
<html>
    <head>
    <title>Page Title</title>
    <link rel="stylesheet" href=" http://code.jquery.
com/mobile/1.0a3/jquery.mobile-1.0a3.min.css" />
        <script src=" http://code.jquery.com/jquery-
1.5.min.js"> </script>
        <script src=" http://code.jquery.com/mobile/1.0a3/
jquery.mobile-1.0a3.min.js"> </script>
    </head>
    <body>
    <div data-role="page">
        <div data-role="header">
            <h1>Page Title</h1>
    </div><!-- /header -->
        <div data-role="content">
            <p>Page content goes here.</p>
    </div><!-- /content -->
        <div data-role="footer">
            <h4>Page Footer</h4>
    </div><!-- /header -->
    </div><!-- /page -->
    </body>
    </html>
```

There are a couple of things worth pointing out in this template. The first is the use of the DIV element. With HTML5 so prevalent in mobile devices why not use the newer HEADER, ARTICLE, SECTION, or FOOTER elements? The reason is progressive enhancement. Older smart phones do not understand the new HTML5 elements. Indeed, the new Windows Phone 7 mobile browser does not support HTML5. The DIV tag is, however, universally supported.

You can save the web page and test it in your web browser. The code is HTML and will work on your desktop. I recommend using Chrome to run your local testing when you want to validate that the HTML/JS works correctly. For real quality testing you will need to run your mobile web pages on different mobile devices.

Creating Pages in Your Mobile Site Using Links

A difference between normal web pages and mobile web pages is the amount of content you can place on the screen. Yes, you can load *The New York Times* website onto your iPhone, but you need to pinch and zoom to read the content. A better solution is to reduce the clutter of the page down to the content you want to present.

A traditional website would have you create many different web pages with a small amount of content on each one. But, we are using jQuery here, so we can tackle the problem of micro-content more efficiently.

In the previous section you saw how you can create a boiler-plate page for jQuery Mobile. Let's take this a step further and create "pages" of content. A page can be structured as a DIV block in jQuery Mobile. Remove the content inside of the BODY elements using the previous boilerplate template (page 14). You are going to add a menu that links to four different pages. The first page is a menu page with links:

```
<!-- Start of first page -->
<div data-role="page" id="menu">
        <div data-role="header">
                <h1>Menu</h1>
        </div><!-- /header -->
        <div data-role="content">
                <p>What vehicles do you like?</p>
                <p><a href="#one">Cars</a></p>
<p><a href="#two">Trains</a></p>
<p><a href="#three">Planes</a></p>
        </div><!-- /content -->
        <div data-role="footer">
                <h4>Page Footer</h4>
        </div><!-- /header -->
</div><!-- /page -->
```

The important part of this block of HTML is the first DIV. Within the element are an ID and data-role properties:

```
data-role="page" id="menu"
```

The data-role defines the content within the DIV element as a "page." This instructs jQuery Mobile to build a web page around the DIV elements. The ID allows you to link up to sections using HREF links.

The menu page is the first page and will then be presented first in the browser. You can add three additional "pages," each with a different ID: Cars, Planes, Trains (see Figure 2.12).

```
<div data-role="page" id="one">
        <div data-role="header">
```

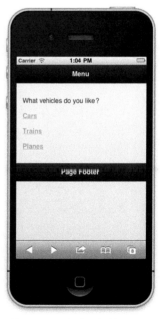

Figure 2.12 A simple jQuery Mobile web app.

```
          <h1>Cars</h1>
   </div><!-- /header -->
   <div data-role="content">
          <p>Content about cars</p>
   </div><!-- /content -->
   <div data-role="footer">
          <h4>Cars</h4>
   </div><!-- /header -->
</div><!-- /page -->
```

Here is the start of the third page:

```
<div data-role="page" id="two">
   <div data-role="header">
          <h1>Trains</h1>
   </div><!-- /header -->
   <div data-role="content">
          <p>Content about trains</p>
   </div><!-- /content -->
   <div data-role="footer">
          <h4>Trains</h4>
   </div><!-- /header -->
</div><!-- /page -->
```

Here is the start of the fourth page:

```
<div data-role="page" id="three">
     <div data-role="header">
       <h1>Planes</h1>
     </div><!-- /header -->
     <div data-role="content">
       <p>Content about planes</p>
     </div><!-- /content -->
     <div data-role="footer">
       <h4>Planes</h4>
     </div><!-- /header -->
</div><!-- /page -->
```

Test the page on your Android or iOS device. When you load the web page you will see three things:

- The menu loads as its own page (you can try to scroll up and down but you will not see anything else).
- When you select a link, the page will transition with an animation sequence as it moves to the new section.
- When you move away from the menu page a back button automatically appears in the top header DIV section.

Each of these DIV elements will load inside the web browser and look like separate web pages. The movement between screens is fluid.

The recommendation of creating multiple pages of content on one screen allows you to eliminate the page load times that cause many mobile devices to appear slow. You can, however, link to external web pages. There is one caveat to this. Links in jQuery

Mobile are treated as Ajax calls. To link outside the current page you are on will require that you clear the use of the # symbol by Ajax. This is done easily enough with the following example:

```
<a href=" http://www.focalpress.com" rel="external">FocalPress
.com</a>
```

You need to include the rel="external" attribute and value. This allows you to link to a web page outside the local page links you have been using up to this point. *But*, jQuery Mobile goes one extra step. Instead of just treating an external link as a link outside your site, jQuery Mobile will apply the page transition animation. This gives you a unique one-up over other popular mobile frameworks. Instead of having all of your website content in one page, you can split up the content over several pages, allowing you to build larger solutions.

Working with Components

Of course, links and pages are just one part of mobile web design. A second challenge many mobile web developers face is the explosion of apps. Unlike web pages, apps for Android, iOS, and other systems are built with complex technologies such as Objective-C, Java, and C#. These technologies allow developers to easily add menu tools, unique lists, and other controls and components not found natively in HTML. Do you think this stops your development with jQuery Mobile? I would like to see it try.

jQuery Mobile is currently shipping with a selection of components. The following components are included in the current Alpha:
• Pages
• Dialogs
• Toolbars
• Buttons
• Content formatting
• Form elements
• List views

Adding and changing a component is not too hard. If you know a little HTML, then you are good to go. Let's look at the page component as an example.

By default, the web page slides back and forth. There are, however, six current page transitions supported. They are:
• Slide
• Slideup
• Slidedown
• Pop
• Fade
• Flip

Adding a custom page transition is a simple modification of an ANCHOR element. For instance, to add 3D flip transition you would add the following data-transition property with a value of "flip".

```
<a href=" http://focalpress.com" data-
transition="flip">focalpress.com</a>
```

The page transition will work with pages using a # or file link.

Adding Headers and Footers to the Page

The previous boilerplate example (page 14) demonstrated how to easily add toolbars such as headers and footers into your page. Toolbars are often the hardest to control when creating content for different screens. The challenge comes in placing content that dynamically scales to different screen sizes. For example, a header toolbar can contain both the header and a button (such as back button). Using jQuery Mobile, the header toolbar will allow you to add a title that stays in the center with a button always staying to the left or right side of the page no matter how large the screen.

The following creates a header toolbar with two buttons on either side of the title.

```
<div data-role="header" data-position="inline">
        <a href="cancel.html" data-icon="delete">Cancel</a>
        <h1>Edit Contact</h1>
        <a href="save.html" data-icon="check">Save</a>
</div>
```

The position of the buttons is defined by the order of the content. The result is a Mobile web page with a centralized title and buttons on the left- and right-hand sides that look and work consistently across devices.

Headers and footers can also be customized into navigation tools. Interactive buttons can be added to a footer that will take you to sections of the screen. This is accomplished with a "navbar" data role. Following is the code for a navbar:

```
<div data-role="navbar">
<ul>
<li><a href="#nav1" class="ui-btn-active">One</a></li>
<li><a href="#nav2">Two</a></li>
</ul>
</div>><!--/navbar-->
```

Again, as you can see with most of the jQuery Mobile code, the navbar is constructed of a simple HTML list wrapped in a DIV tag. Properties such as the ui-btn-active can be set to identify a button that should be selected, as shown in Figure 2.13.

When you select a button and go to a second screen within the same page, jQuery Mobile is smart enough to automatically add a back button to the header.

Figure 2.13 jQuery Mobile navigation buttons.

Working with Navbars

A back button is good for one interaction, but what happens when you need to offer two or more buttons to a user? In this instance, you need to use a Navbar to add navigation buttons.

For instance, the following HTML adds three screens in one HTML page. You have the main screen and two sample screens you can link to from the navbar. Add the code and see how the navigation automatically adds back buttons. The following code sets up the page:

```
<div data-role="page">
       <div data-role="header">
              <h1>Navigation</h1>
              </div><!-- /header -->
              <div data-role="content">
                     Navigation page
              </div><!-- /content -->
              <div data-role="footer">
```

The navbar is placed within the footer. In this example you are adding a navbar with two buttons that reference content within this page:

```
<div data-role="navbar">
              <ul>
                     <li><a href="#nav1" class="ui-btn-
active">One</a></li>
                     <li><a href="#nav2">Two</a></li>
              </ul>
       </div><!-- /navbar -->
</div><!-- /footer -->
</div><!-- /page -->
```

The following is the page the left hand button references in the navbar:

```
<div data-role="page" id="nav1">
       <div data-role="header">
              <h1>Nav Screen 1</h1>
       </div><!-- /header -->
       <div data-role="content">
Screen for Navigation One </div><!-- /content -->
       <div data-role="footer">
              <h4>Additional Footer information</h4>
       </div><!-- /header -->
</div><!-- /page -->
```

The following is the page the right-hand button references in the navbar:

```
<div data-role="page" id="nav2">
       <div data-role="header">
              <h1>Nav Screen 2</h1>
```

```
        </div><!-- /header -->
        <div data-role="content">
Screen for Navigation Two
</div><!-- /content -->
        <div data-role="footer">
                <h4>Additional Footer information</h4>
        </div><!-- /header -->
</div><!-- /page -->
```

Remember to add the SCRIPT and CSS references for jQuery Mobile. Test and run the code on your device.

Making Footers and Headers Persistent

A common user interface design technique is to keep the header and footer at the top and bottom of the screen. You can use jQuery Mobile to accomplish this by simply adding data-position="fixed" to the header or footer. This will force the header to be flush with the top and the footer to be flush with the bottom. Here is an example (illustrated in Figure 2.14):

```
<div data-role="page">
<div data-role="header" data-position="fixed">
<h1>Navigation</h1>
</div><!-- /header -->
<div data-role="content">
```

Here is a list view to add additional data to the screen:

```
<ul data-role="listview" data-dividertheme="d"
style="margin-top: 0;">
    <li data-role="list-divider">Royal Family</li>
    <li><a href="#nav1">Henry VIII</a></li>
    <li><a href="#nav1">George V</a></li>
    <li><a href="#nav1">Prince of Wales</a></li>
    <li><a href="#nav1">Elizabeth I</a></li>
    <li><a href="#nav1">Elizabeth II</a></li>
    <li data-role="list-divider">Prime Ministers</li>
    <li><a href="#nav2">Winston Churchill</a></li>
    <li><a href="#nav2">Tony Blair</a></li>
    <li><a href="#nav2">David Cameron</a></li>
</ul>
</div><!-- /content -->
```

Figure 2.14 The header and footer bars are fixed on the screen.

Following is a footer section. Notice that the "fixed" attribute has been added. You will observe that as you select the screen to scroll, the fixed footer will fade out, giving you more space to flick your finger.

```
<div data-role="footer" data-position="fixed">
<div data-role="navbar">
<ul>
<li><a href="#nav1" class="ui-btn-active">Royals</a></li>
<li><a href="#nav2">Leaders</a></li>
</ul>
```

```
</div><!--/navbar -->
</div><!--/footer -->
</div><!--/page -->
<div data-role="page" id="nav1" data-position="fixed">
<div data-role="header">
<h1>Royal Family</h1>
</div><!--/header -->
<div data-role="content">
<p>Members and relatives of the British Royal Family
historically represented the monarch in various places
throughout the British Empire, sometimes for extended
periods as viceroys, or for specific ceremonies or events.
Today, they often perform ceremonial and social duties
throughout the United Kingdom and abroad on behalf of the
UK, but, aside from the monarch, have no constitutional role
in the affairs of government. This is the same for the other
realms of the Commonwealth though the family there acts on
behalf of, is funded by, and represents the sovereign of
that particular state, and not the United Kingdom.</P>
</div><!-- /content -->
```

A footer does not need to be used with just lists. Here the footer is fixed on standard HTML:

```
<div data-role="footer" data-position="fixed">
<h4>Royal Family</h4>
</div><!--/header -->
</div><!--/page -->
```

Notice that we also have a fixed header in this sample. Unlike the footer, which disappears, the header stays with the content as you scroll.

```
<div data-role="page" id="nav2" data-position="fixed">
<div data-role="header">
<h1>Prime Ministers</h1>
</div><!--/header -->
<div data-role="content">
The Prime Minister of the United Kingdom of Great Britain
and Northern Ireland is the Head of Her Majesty's Government
in the United Kingdom. The Prime Minister and Cabinet
(consisting of all the most senior ministers, who are
government department heads) are collectively accountable
for their policies and actions to the Sovereign, to
Parliament, to their political party and ultimately to the
electorate. The current Prime Minister, David Cameron, was
appointed on 11 May 2010.</div><!--/content -->
<div data-role="footer" data-position="fixed">
<h4>Prime Minister</h4>
</div><!--/header -->
</div><!--/page -->
```

Now, without using custom Objective-C you can add fixed headers and footers to your pages.

Figure 2.15 The jQuery Mobile dialog box.

Working with Dialogs

The Page component also allows you to add custom CSS pop-up dialog boxes using the data-rel property. For instance, the following will load a web page into a pop-up dialog box:

```
<a href="dialog.html" data-rel="dialog">Open dialog</a>
```

Using this method allows you to load any custom message into your dialog box, as shown in Figure 2.15. You do need two sections to a dialog when posting a dialog in the same page. The first section displays a link to the dialog, as shown here:

```
<div data-role="page">
     <div data-role="header">
          <h1>Dialog Box</h1>
     </div><!-- /header -->
     <div data-role="content">
          <a href="#dialogPopUp" data-rel="dialog"
data-role="button">Open dialog</a>
     </div><!-- /content -->
     <div data-role="footer">
          <h4>Page Footer</h4>
     </div><!-- /header -->
</div><!-- /page -->
```

You can see in the HREF for the Open Dialog button that there is a link to a local section. The following is a markup that will appear in the dialog box:

```
<div data-role="page" id="dialogPopUp">
     <div data-role="header">
          <h1>Dialog Title</h1>
     </div><!-- /header -->
     <div data-role="content">
          This is a dialog box
     </div><!-- /content -->
     <div data-role="footer">
          <h4>Additional Footer information</h4>
     </div><!-- /header -->
</div><!-- /page -->
```

The inclusion of the footer is optional, but you must include the header. Without the header, the automatic inclusion of a close button will *not* appear.

Working with Lists

There is a lot of data on the web. Lists are effective tools you can use to manage large amounts of data. We have already used lists in a couple of the earlier examples, but now let's get down and dirty with them.

At their core, lists are just, well... lists. One of the oldest HTML elements is the LIST element (you can see it in web pages that go back to the early 1990s). Here is a simple list using standard HTML, illustrated in Figure 2.16:

```
<ul>
<li><a href="#nav1">Henry VIII</a></li>
<li><a href="#nav1">George V</a></li>
<li><a href="#nav1">Prince of Wales</a></li>
<li><a href="#nav1">Elizabeth I</a></li>
<li><a href="#nav1">Elizabeth II</a></li>
</ul>
```

In jQuery Mobile you can convert this simple list into a gorgeous, APP-like list by adding one set of attributes to the open UL tag. The data-role attribute will tell jQuery Mobile to redraw the list to look like and perform as if it were a native app, as follows:

```
<ul data-role="listview" style="margin-top: 0;">
<li><a href="#nav1">Henry VIII</a></li>
<li><a href="#nav1">George V</a></li>
<li><a href="#nav1">Prince of Wales</a></li>
<li><a href="#nav1">Elizabeth I</a></li>
<li><a href="#nav1">Elizabeth II</a></li>
</ul>
```

Figure 2.16 A basic list.

That's it, just 20 characters and you have a formatted list. This is code you can tweet!

Outside of the basic list, jQuery gives you the option to extend the core list. For instance, the following will add dividers to the lists:

```
<ul data-role="listview" data-dividertheme="d"
style="margin-top: 0;">
    <li data-role="list-divider">Royal Family</li>
    <li><a href="#home">Henry VIII</a></li>
    <li><a href="#home">George V</a></li>
    <li><a href="#home">Prince of Wales</a></li>
    <li><a href="#home">Elizabeth I</a></li>
    <li><a href="#home">Elizabeth II</a></li>
    <li data-role="list-divider">Prime Ministers</li>
    <li><a href="#home">Winston Churchill</a></li>
    <li><a href="#home">Tony Blair</a></li>
    <li><a href="#home">David Cameron</a></li>
</ul>
```

Dividers are added by including the attribute data-dividertheme="d" in the opening UL tag and including a special list item where you want your divider to appear (<li **data-role="list-divider"**>Royal Family</li>), as illustrated in Figure 2.17.

Figure 2.17 List with dividers.

Figure 2.18 List with data in right-hand side bubbles.

Data bubbles can also be added to each list item, as shown in Figure 2.18. In the following example the reign of each member of the British Royal Family is added to a bubble immediately to the right of each item.

```
<ul data-role="listview" style="margin-top: 0;">
<li><a href="#nav1">Henry VIII <span class="ui-li-count">
Reign 37 Years</span></a></li>
<li><a href="#nav1">George V <span class="ui-li-count">
Reign 25 Years</span></a></li>
<li><a href="#nav1">Prince of Wales <span class="ui-li-
count">N/A</span></a></li>
<li><a href="#nav1">Elizabeth I <span class="ui-li-count">
Reign 44 Years</span></a></li>
<li><a href="#nav1">Elizabeth II<span class="ui-li-count">
Reign since 1952</span></a></li>
</ul>
```

The fourth type of list is a complex list where you can add links, images, and text within an LI element; for example:

```
<ul data-role="listview" style="margin-top: 0;">
<li>
<img src="http://img.freebase.com/api/trans/image_thumb/
en/henry_viii_of_england?pad=1&errorid=%2Ffreebase%2Fno_
image_png&maxheight=64&mode=fillcropmid&maxwidth=64"/>
<h3><a href="index.html">Henry VIII</a></h3>
<p>Reign 37 Years</p>
<a href="#home">Details</a>
</li>
```

In this example you can see that HTML code is placed between each LI element. The first piece is an image. To keep your layout consistent, make sure you use the same size image. Each of the following LI items have an image that is 64×64 pixels in PNG format, as shown in Figure 2.19.

The second item is a title with an HREF link. Following the title is a section where you can add a paragraph text.

The final element is an HREF link with the word "details". When you preview this page you will not see the word "details" because it will be replaced with a custom arrow icon.

Figure 2.19 List with images.

```
<li>
<img src="http://www.iwise.com/authorIcons/15/King_
George%20V_64x64.png" />
<h3><a href="index.html">George V</a></h3>
<p>Reign 25 Years</p>
<a href="#home">Details</a>
</li>
<li>
<img src="http://img.freebase.com/api/trans/image_thumb/
en/prince:of_wales_secondary_school?pad=1&errorid=%2Ffreebase
%2Fno_image_png&maxheight=64&mode=fillcropmid&maxwidth=64"/>
<h3><a href="index.html">Prince of Wales</a></h3>
```

```
<p>Reign N/A</p>
<a href="#home">Details</a>
</li>
<li>
<img src="http://www.iwise.com/authorIcons/13846/
Elizabeth%20I%20of%20England_64x64.png" />
<h3><a href="index.html">Elizabeth I</a></h3>
<p>Reign 44 Years</p>
<a href="#home">Details</a>
</li>
<li>
<img src="http://www.iwise.com/authorIcons/9098/
Elizabeth%20II_64x64.png" />
<h3><a href="index.html">Elizabeth II</a></h3>
<p>Reign Since 1952</p>
<a href="#home">Details</a>
</li>
</ul>
```

This is a complex looking list, but not really too complex to write. The result is that you give your audience a list with a lot of data.

Adding Custom Icons to Buttons, Lists, and Navigation

There are many different types of data-icons you can add. They include:
- Left arrow: data-icon="arrow-l"
- Right arrow: data-icon="arrow-r"
- Up arrow: data-icon="arrow-u"
- Down arrow: data-icon="arrow-d"
- Delete: data-icon="delete"
- Plus: data-icon="plus"
- Minus: data-icon="minus"
- Check: data-icon="check"
- Gear: data-icon="gear"
- Refresh: data-icon="refresh"
- Forward: data-icon="forward"
- Back: data-icon="back"
- Grid: data-icon="grid"
- Star: data icon-"star"
- Alert: data-icon="alert"
- Info: data-icon="info"
- Home: data-icon="home"
- Search: data-icon="search"

The following navigation bar shows how you can add custom buttons using the data-icon reference:

```
<div data-role="footer">
<div data-role="navbar">
<ul>
<li><a href="#" data-icon="grid" data-iconpos="top">
Summary</a></li>
<li><a href="#" data-icon="star" class="ui-btn-active"
data-iconpos="top">Favs</a></li>
```

Figure 2.20 You can add custom icons such as those found at glyphish.com.

```
<li><a href="#" data-icon="gear" data-
iconpos="top">Setup</a></li>
</ul>
</div><!--/navbar -->
</div><!--/footer -->
```

In addition, you can create your own icons and have those inserted. A very popular set of icons can be found at *http://glyphish.com/*, as shown in Figure 2.20. There are two parts to adding custom icons. The first is creating the graphics and then adding the CSS as shown here:

```
<style type="text/css">
.nav-glyphish-example .ui-btn .ui-btn-inner { padding-
top: 40px !important; }
    .nav-glyphish-example .ui-btn .ui-icon { width:
30px!important; height: 30px!important; margin-left: -15px
!important; box-shadow: none!important; -moz-box-shadow:
none!important; -webkit-box-shadow: none!important;
-webkit-border-radius: none !important; border-radius:
none !important; }
    #chat .ui-icon { background: url(glyphish-icons/09-
chat2.png) 50% 50% no-repeat; background-size: 24px
22px; }
    #email .ui-icon { background: url(glyphish-icons/18-
envelope.png) 50% 50% no-repeat; background-size: 24px
16px; }
    #login .ui-icon { background: url(glyphish-icons/30-
key.png) 50% 50% no-repeat; background-size: 12px 26px; }
    #beer .ui-icon { background: url(glyphish-icons/88-
beermug.png) 50% 50% no-repeat; background-size: 22px
27px; }
    #coffee .ui-icon { background: url(glyphish-icons/100-
coffee.png) 50% 50% no-repeat; background-size: 20px 24px; }
    #skull .ui-icon { background: url(glyphish-icons/21-
skull.png) 50% 50% no-repeat; background-size: 22px 24px; }
</style>
```

The second section is adding the custom icons to list items. In the following you will see each LI has an ID, which matches the CSS class with the data-icon set to custom.

```
<div data-role="footer" class="nav-glyphish-example">
<div data-role="navbar" class="nav-glyphish-example"
data-grid="d">
<ul>
<li><a href="#" id="chat" data-icon="custom">Chat</a>
</li>
<li><a href="#" id="email" data-icon="custom">Email
</a></li>
<li><a href="#" id="skull" data-icon="custom">Danger
</a></li>
```

```
    <li><a href="#" id="beer" data-icon="custom">Beer</a>
</li>
    <li><a href="#" id="coffee" data-icon="custom">Coffee
</a></li>
    </ul>
    </div>
    </div>
```

The same model for applying custom icons can be used for buttons, headers, footers, and navigation menus.

Gesture-Driven Events

As you will have noticed, the components are sensitive to gestures: taps, swipes, and hold events. There are five gestures currently supported:
- Tap: Quick tap on the screen
- Taphold: Hold your finger down
- Swipe: Swipe in any direction more than 30 px
- Swipeleft: Swipe left more than 30 px
- Swiperight: Swipe right more than 30 px

Gestures are supported only in browsers such as Mobile Safari and Android. Older browsers ignore the gesture and treat taps as if they were mouse clicks.

There are some gestures clearly not supported at this time such as multitouch gestures (two-finger tap, etc.) and pinch-to-zoom style gestures. It is likely you will see this in future releases or as plug-ins to jQuery Mobile.

Extending jQuery Mobile with Plug-ins and Custom JavaScript

In many respects, jQuery Mobile is a super-sized plug-in for the core jQuery framework. When you start thinking of jQuery Mobile in these terms, you realize that most jQuery plug-ins should work within your mobile device. The following sections describe several essential plug-ins. There are, however, hundreds of jQuery plug-ins you can use that we do not cover. For more information on jQuery plug-ins, check out *http://plugins.jquery.com*.

Form Validation for jQuery Mobile

There is a good chance that, as a Mobile web developer, you will need to write a form or two. Heck, you will probably have to write hundreds. Wouldn't it be nice if you could control the content that is entered into the form?

jQuery plug-ins to the rescue! The Validate plug-in allows you to do all the heavy work for form control such as:

- Requiring a field to be filled
- Checking that the e-mail is correctly written
- Checking that the credit card number is entered correctly
- Checking if the minimum number of characters were entered
- Checking whether too many characters were entered
- Checking whether the value entered needed to match another value on the screen

You can write all of this out using JavaScript or use a server side-script to test for this, but I am guessing you will not be able to find anything that is as easy to use as the Validate plug-in for jQuery. So, enough jabbering from me, let's get into the code.

Setting Up Your Page for Form Validation

The first step you need to take for standard form validation is to link the jQuery and Validate plug-in files to your web page. Add the following code in your web page HEAD element:

```
<script src="http://code.jquery.com/jquery-latest.js">
</script>
    <script type="text/javascript" src="http://dev.jquery.
com/view/trunk/plugins/validate/jquery.validate.js"></script>
```

Now you only need a web form to validate against. A normal web form looks something like this:

```
<form id="yourForm" method="get" action="">
 <fieldset>
  <p>
   <label>Name</label>
   <input id="name" size="25"/>
  </p>
  <p>
   <label">E-Mail</label>
   <input id="email" size="25" />
  </p>
  <p>
 <label">Your comment</label>
 <textarea id="comment" cols="22"></textarea>
  </p>
  <p>
   <input class="submit" type="submit" value="Submit"/>
  </p>
 </fieldset>
</form>
```

What you would like to do is make sure that all the fields are required. The first step is to create a link between jQuery and the form in the HTML. If you look, you will see that the form has an ID of "yourForm". You can reference this ID using JavaScript. Add the following script in the HEAD element of your page after the links to jQuery and the Validate plug-in:

```
<script>
  $(document).ready(function(){
    $("# yourForm ").validate();
  });
</script>
```

Notice on line 3 how you link to the form ID we created? That's all the JavaScript you need to write.

The Validate plug-in ships with a large number of built-in common validation rules. You add them to the Class attribute in a field. For instance, the following will make the INPUT element be required:

```
<input id="name" size="25" class="required"/>
```

You can test to see if the new validation works. Save your web page and open it in a web browser. Select the Submit button. You will see the warning, "This field is required," in red text to the right of the name field. Click inside of the name field and start typing. As soon as you enter in any content the warning message goes away.

What if you want the field to be required and formatted to a specific type of content, such as an e-mail address? You can do that by adding in two or more class references. The following example makes the e-mail field both required and formatted to an e-mail regular expression:

```
<input id="email" size="25" class="required email"/>
```

Right out of the box, you can see that adding validation rules is very simple.

Customizing Your Error Message

What if you want something different? For instance, you want the message to change for different errors. To do this, you will need to download and use a local copy of the Validate plug-in. Now is the time to modify the code. *Warning*: JavaScript is now in session, folks.

There are two parts to modifying a validation rule:
• Name
• Method

The validation name is the ID you will use in the HTML Class attribute in your web page.

The validation method is the rule that tests if the content meets certain criteria (such as valid e-mail format, credit card, or date).

Open your local copy of the Validate plug-in and find the section that starts with "message." You will see all the different default validation types you can use defined as a name followed by the error message if the validation rule is not met. The section will look like this:

```
messages: {
            required: "This field is required.",
            remote: "Please fix this field.",
            email: "Please enter a valid email address.",
            url: "Please enter a valid URL.",
            date: "Please enter a valid date.",
            dateISO: "Please enter a valid date (ISO).",
            dateDE: "Bitte geben Sie ein gÃ¼ltiges Datum
ein.",
            number: "Please enter a valid number.",
            numberDE: "Bitte geben Sie eine Nummer ein.",
            digits: "Please enter only digits",
            creditcard: "Please enter a valid credit card
number.",
            equalTo: "Please enter the same value again.",
            accept: "Please enter a value with a valid
extension.",
            maxlength: $.format("Please enter no more
than {0} characters."),
            minlength: $.format("Please enter at least
{0} characters."),
            rangelength: $.format("Please enter a
value between {0} and {1} characters long."),
            range: $.format("Please enter a value between
{0} and {1}."),
            max: $.format("Please enter a value less
than or equal to {0}."),
            min: $.format("Please enter a value greater
than or equal to {0}.")
            }
```

There is a corresponding method for each name listed. Here is an example of the "required" method:

```
required: function(value, element, param) {
if ( !this.depend(param, element) )
        return "dependency-mismatch";
switch( element.nodeName.toLowerCase() ) {
        case 'select':
var options = $("option:selected", element);
    return options.length > 0 && ( element.type == "select-
multiple" || ($.browser.msie && !(options[0].attributes['value'].
specified) ? options[0].text : options[0].value).length > 0);
        case 'input':
                if ( this.checkable(element) )
                    return this.getLength(value, element) > 0;
```

DEVELOPING WEBSITES WITH jQUERY MOBILE **99**

```
        default:
                return $.trim(value).length > 0;
        }
    }
```

This is where the code is located. Now, let's talk about creating a custom rule.

Creating a Custom Message

So, what do you do if you want to create your own custom message? The easiest way to get started is to create an alternative copy of the "required" field.

1. You are going to create a new rule that is called customMessage. Add the following (the modified code is in bold):

```
messages: {
        required: "This field is required.",
        customMessage: "This is a custom message!",
        remote: "Please fix this field.",
        email: "Please enter a valid email address.",
```

2. Locate the classRuleSettings section and add a reference to your new rule.

```
classRuleSettings: {
                required: {required: true},
                customMessage: { customMessage: true},
                email: {email: true},
                url: {url: true},
                date: {date: true},
                dateISO: {dateISO: true},
                dateDE: {dateDE: true},
                number: {number: true},
                numberDE: {numberDE: true},
                digits: {digits: true},
                creditcard: {creditcard: true}
        }
```

3. Create a method for your new rule. Here we are just copying the function of the default required method, but with a reference to our customMessage name:

```
customMessage: function(value, element, param) {
if (!this.depend(param, element) )
        return "dependency-mismatch";
switch(element.nodeName.toLowerCase() ) {
        case 'select':
                var options = $("option:selected",
element);
                return options.length > 0 && (
element.type == "select-multiple" || ($.browser.msie &&
!(options[0].attributes['value'].specified) ? options[0].
text : options[0].value).length > 0);
```

```
                              case 'input':
                                      if ( this.checkable(element) )
                                      return this.getLength(value, element) > 0;
                              default:
                                      return $.trim(value).length > 0;
                              }

                    }
```

4. Save the modified Validate JS file.
5. Go to your HTML form and add the Class attribute custom-Message. Test your file in your web browser. You should see a custom message.

This section covered only the basics of the Validate plug-in. You can do a lot more, such as add rules. Check it out and let me know what kind of custom rules you create.

Template, Data Link, and Globalization Plug-ins for jQuery

When you think Open Source, the name that does not leap to mind is Microsoft, but it should. Over the last few years Microsoft has changed its approach to Open Source projects. This is clearly demonstrated with its commitment to jQuery.

Back in May 2010, Microsoft stated that it would bring three new features to jQuery: Templates, Data Link, and Globalization. On October 4, 2010, Microsoft delivered on its promise. You can find the news release over at the jQuery blog, *http://blog.jquery.com/2010/10/04/new-official-jquery-plugins-provide-templating-data-linking-and-globalization/*, as shown in Figure 2.21.

Each of these three plug-ins is very broad in scope. Here is a brief summary of each, followed by links to more detailed tutorials:

*   Templates: As the name suggests, Templates enables you to template your data in a logical structure.
*   Data Link: This plug-in allows more effective data synchronization capabilities.
*   Globalization: This plug-in allows you to add globalization in over 350 cultures.

Here are some great tutorials from the Microsoft folks which explain how each of these plug-ins work:

*   jQuery Templates and Data-Link: *http://weblogs.asp.net/scottgu/archive/2010/05/07/jquery-templates-and-data-linking-and-microsoft-contributing-to-jquery.aspx*
*   Introducing jQuery Templates: *www.borismoore.com/2010/09/introducing-jquery-templates-1-first.html*
*   jQuery Templates in the wild: *www.jamessenior.com/2010/09/30/jquery-templating-in-the-wild/*

Figure 2.21 jQuery's official blog.

What is very interesting about Microsoft's contribution is that the new plug-ins must adhere to the same licensing as jQuery itself. Is this a PR scheme from Microsoft or a genuine contribution to a great Open Source project? I am not sure I care; I am just delighted to see new and awesome tools available for the jQuery community. Keep up the good work, Microsoft.

jQuery + Google Analytics = Very Useful Plug-in

Tracking activity on your website is essential. When you track user activity you can validate the success of your content or a campaign. This is exactly the same for mobile web development. Google is a leader in website analytics. With Google Analytics (Figure 2.22) you can track where on your site your customer is going, how long they are there, and which browser they are using. Google has even given mobile developers an additional bounty in that you can separate mobile traffic from desktop computer traffic.

Figure 2.22 Google Analytics website.

A group called Aktagon Ltd. has created a Google Analytics plug-in that is essential if you want to track activity on your website. You can see a brief demo here: *http://aktagon.com/projects/jquery/google-analytics.html*. The code is available at this site: http://github.com/christianhellsten/jquery-google-analytics.

You will need some Google Analytics experience to use the code. The role of Google Analytics is to allow you to track users as they move through your website. This is very similar to any of the dozens of website statistic tools on the market. The types of tracking you can complete include:

• Activity on a page
• Links selected
• Event actions (such as submitting a form with a button)

The problem with Google Analytics is that it gets to be annoying as you add more complex tracking activities. This is where the AKTAGON plug-in really shines. The uncompressed JS file can be copied from this page: *http://github.com/christianhellsten/jquery-google-analytics/blob/master/jquery.google-analytics.js*.

Now let's step through what you need to do to add this to your site.

1. Create a new web page and add the usual links to jQuery:

```
<script type="text/javascript" src=" jquery.min.js">
</script>
```

2. Link to the Google Analytics plug-in:

```
<script src="jquery.google-analytics.js" type="text/
javascript"></script>
```

3. You are almost ready to get the basic functionality working. All you now need to do is add a reference to your unique Google Analytics code in the HEAD element on your page:

```
<script type="text/javascript">
    $.trackPage('UA-XXXXXXX-1', {onload:true})
</script>
```

The value in the parentheses is where you add your UA ID. The curly brackets are really interesting. Here you can add additional values. The following are supported:

- onload (Boolean): If false, the Google Analytics code is loaded when this method is called instead of on window.onload. The default is true.
- status_code: The HTTP status code of the current server response. If this is set to something other than 200 then the page is tracked as an error page. For more details refer to *www.google .com/support/analytics/bin/answer.py?hl=en&answer=86927.*
- callback: Function to be executed after the Google Analytics code is loaded and initialized.

At this point you are done. The whole script should look like this:

```
<html>
  <head>
    <title>jQuery Google Analytics Plug-in Examples</title>
    <script type="text/javascript" src="jquery.min.js">
</script>
    <script src="jquery.google-analytics.js" type="text/
javascript"></script>
    <script type="text/javascript">
     $.trackPage(UA-xxxxx-1, {status_code: 404})
    </script>
  </head>
<body>
Enter content for your page
</body>
</html>
```

That's it. If you have worked with Google's own JavaScript code, then you already know this is much cleaner.

Of course there is more you can do. One of the things you can do with Google Analytics is create categories to track different types of data. For instance, you may want to call content you have on the eCommerce or mainContent pages to help sort through all the data more easily. Well, the good folks over at AKTAGON have added the ability to categorize your content easily.

Under the $.trackPage script add the following line to include a new category:

```
$('.eCommerce a').track({
    category : 'eCommerceTraffic'
});
```

This code will pass any link selected within a section using the eCommerce class back to Google Analytics with the category eCommerceTraffic associated with it. This allows for more comprehensive tracking in your Google Analytics code.

An example of the HTML with the correct class name is:

```
<div class=" eCommerce ">
<p>lorem ipsum - blah - blah - blah</p>
    <a href="http://www.focalpress.com">This link will
have a category associated with it when you click on it</a>
    </div>
```

Something I learned as I dug through the Google Analytics plug-in is that you can send information back to Google on links as you move your mouse over but do not select. This is very cool because you can see if people are even thinking of selecting a link on a page, or if they simply do not even see it. This is how you do it with the plug-in:

```
$(document).ready(function(){
    $('a#hover').track({event_name: 'mouseover'})
    });
<a href="www.google.com" id="hover">Hover over me</a>
```

All in all, this is a very cool plug-in that makes it much easier to access complex functionality in Google Analytics.

Extending jQuery Mobile with Custom Themes

The layout and presentation of elements in jQuery Mobile on the screen is accomplished using Cascading Style Sheets (CSS). To this end you can go in and rewrite the CSS styles that are in the default setup.

You may want to wait until the jQuery UI ThemeRoller is integrated into jQuery Mobile, which is preferable, as shown in Figure 2.23.

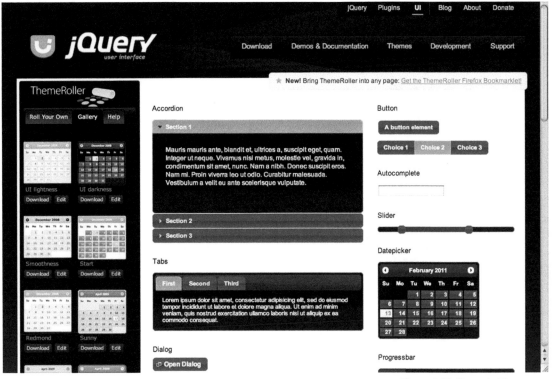

Figure 2.23 jQuery's UI ThemeRoller.

The jQuery UI team extended the functionality of its visual design elements to allow you to easily change the color schemes of widgets to match your corporate brand. This same model is also coming to jQuery Mobile. Fingers crossed, by the time you read this the jQuery Mobile team will have added ThemeRoller integration.

Converting Your jQuery Website into an App Using PhoneGap

You have spent all this time building a great website using jQuery Mobile. What about real apps? You can choose to learn Objective-C, Java, and C#, or you can leverage your knowledge of jQuery and use it as the foundation for your mobile apps.

A clever tool that is gaining a growing user community is PhoneGap. Essentially, PhoneGap is an Open Source project that allows you to use HTML, CSS, and JavaScript to build real-world native apps for iOS (Tablet and handheld), Android, BlackBerry, Symbian, and Palm. Yes, you heard me, real apps, not just web pages (see Figure 2.24).

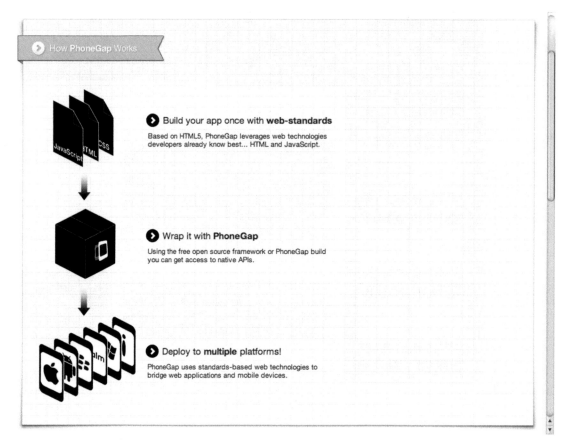

Figure 2.24 How PhoneGap works.

The way PhoneGap works is that it sits as a project inside your development environment. For instance, for iOS development, PhoneGap is a special project type in Xcode. When you load the project type you are able to build your entire iOS project using HTML. Extensions in PhoneGap allow you to tap into core features within the device that are outside of HTML. For instance, you may want to use the microphone to record a message. HTML does not allow you to do that today, but extensions in PhoneGap do allow you to do this.

PhoneGap recommends jQuery Mobile as the first choice in supported mobile frameworks. Check it out over at *www.phonegap.com*. I use PhoneGap a lot for the simple reason that I can take a website developed with jQuery Mobile and port it to all the popular smart phones without needing to learn a lot of different languages. We will be getting into PhoneGap support later, but I thought it worthwhile letting you know now.

Keeping Up to Date on the Latest News and Getting Involved

Twitter is a great way to get news instantly. I particularly like getting updates as text messages to my phone.

There are some great jQuery accounts you should be subscribing to:

- @jquery: The official word from *the* source
- @smashingmag: They have some great jQuery articles
- @jqtouch: One of the best jQuery plug-ins for mobile frameworks
- @usejquery: Nice tidbits
- @jquerypodcast: Know when your favorite podcast is updated
- @jquerybot: Lots of great information
- @matthewadavid: Well, it's my tweet and I'm gonna think it's great!

Let me know if I have missed any from this list—send me a tweet!

If you are also finding that you are using jQuery Mobile frequently, why not get involved with the open source program? If developers did not write jQuery code, users did not test it, and designers did not implement jQuery then the product simply would not exist. As a group, we have made jQuery the success story it is today.

Here are some things you can do:

- The first step is to simply start using jQuery—add the jQuery library to a web page, an app, or something, but just get your hands dirty with the code.
- Find a bug? Report it! The jQuery team has a great site dedicated to bug tracking: *http://docs.jquery.com/How_to_Report_Bugs*.
- Want to chat about jQuery with like-minded people? Jump on the IRC or forums: *http://forum.jquery.com/developing-jquery-core*.
- Extend jQuery with your own plug-ins and contribute the plug-ins back to the community: *http://plugins.jquery.com/*.
- Feeling really brave? Then fix some of the bugs in the core library—this section has a whole piece on how to download the latest code: *http://docs.jquery.com/Getting_Involved*.

There you are, some simple ways to get involved with the jQuery community.

Beyond Alpha

A lot of work has clearly gone into the current Alpha release of jQuery Mobile. With that said, it is clearly still an alpha. Sometimes the code does not execute correctly and the spinning "loading" symbol can get annoying. With that said, I have high hopes for jQuery Mobile. Both jQuery and jQuery UI are solid and dependable frameworks.

Future enhancements you can expect to see coming to jQuery Mobile include:

- Support for the jQuery UI ThemeRoller, allowing you to create your own custom styles
- Support for tablet layouts such as Apple's iPad popovers and side menus

Additional features I would like to see include enhanced gesture support and access to HTML5 APIs in iOS and Android such as geolocation.

If you have been waiting to jump into the mobile web design world then your wait is over. Though not fully baked, jQuery Mobile gives you a framework that would otherwise make mobile web development very difficult.

PROJECT: BUILDING A MOBILE WEBSITE USING jQUERY MOBILE

The focus of this project is to provide you with a complete jQuery Mobile website. To up the ante and give you a little more, I am also going to show how you can incorporate a second framework that dynamically pulls in external data to automatically populate your screens.

What You Will Need

To get started with this project you will need to download the files from *www.visualizetheweb.com*. The files for this project are contained in a ZIP file that you can extract on your desktop.

All you need to build the project are the following project files:

- Index.html
- History.html
- Images folder (with one image)
- SpryAssets (containing two JavaScripts and one CSS document)

Setting Up jQuery Mobile

Unlike a normal website where you have individual pages for content, jQuery Mobile uses a method where all the screens for a website are in a single document. The illusion of moving from screen to screen is created using JavaScript.

Let's get started with the main document you will create. Open the file named index.html, as shown in Figure P2.1.

This project uses the CDN version of jQuery Mobile. The advantage the CDN version provides is that the files are hosted on a different website and do not use your own web server resources.

Figure P2.1 The first screen in the jQuery Mobile app.

As you will see, the files point to document hosted on jQuery.com:

```
<!DOCTYPE html>
<html>
<head>
<title>Pocket History - Ancient Egypt</title>
<link rel="stylesheet" href="http://code.jquery.
com/mobile/1.0a4.1/jquery.mobile-1.0a4.1.min.css" />
<script src="http://code.jquery.com/jquery-
1.5.2.min.js"></script>
<script src="http://code.jquery.com/
mobile/1.0a4.1/jquery.mobile-1.0a4.1.min.js"></script>
</head>
<body>
```

The documents you are pointing to include jQuery, jQuery Mobile, and the jQuery Mobile CSS Theme.

The BODY element is where you will place the visual content. Screens are managed within DIV elements on the page with a special Data-role attribute labeled "page". Each "page" is a screen that displays content. To navigate from screen to screen you must provide a name for the screen in the ID attribute. Here you will see that the ID is "menu":

```
<!-- Start of first page -->
<div data-role="page" id="menu" data-theme="e">
  <div data-role="header">
    <h1>Ancient Egypt Rocks</h1>
  </div>
<!-- /header -->
```

The preceding code is the content that appears as the "header" section for a screen. You will see that the Data-theme attribute has been added to include support for the jQuery Mobile swatch labeled "e" to give a yellow theme to the application.

The following is the content that appears on the screen. The Data-role attribute in the first DIV element defines this section as "content."

There are two pieces of content on the screen: a graphic and a button. The button points to a screen called "history":

```
<div data-role="content">
  <p align="center"> <img src="images/head.png" ></P>
  <p align="center"><a href="#history" data-
role="button" >What are Hieroglyphics?</a></p>
</div>
  <!-- /content -->
</div>
  <!-- /page -->
```

The screen labeled #history contains a list that points to additional information. You can manually create additional screens or you can use the following technique to dynamically build your screen with JavaScript.

Pulling in Dynamic Data

Taking advantage of Ajax techniques to pull data into your applications dynamically can save you a lot of work. This project demonstrates how you can use additional Ajax libraries to supplement jQuery to manage complex data.

The toolset you will use is Adobe's Spry framework. The Spry framework is built into Adobe's Dreamweaver but you can also download the files here: *http://labs.adobe.com/technologies/spry/*.

Adobe's Spry has a lot of features that allow for animation, content control, and forms management. The single task you want Spry to perform is dynamically creating data on the screen. There are two types of structured data supported by Spry: XML and HTML tables. For this project you are using an HTML table for the structure data.

Open the web document named history.html. The main structure of the document is a table with rows for each entry.

The TABLE element is a normal table. There is an ID attribute in the table. A web page can have many TABLE elements. The ID is used to instruct Spry which TABLE to use. The ID attribute in this project is named "history":

```
<table width="100%" border="1" id="history">
```

Following the ID is the first row of data. Spry takes the first row and assumes that each entry within the TD elements is a column header. Later, you will use the column headers to create a dynamic template.

```
<tr>
  <td>LeadIn</td>
  <td>Content</td>
  <td>Author</td>
  <td>Order</td>
  <td>Source</td>
</tr>
```

The second and all following rows each represent content. The structure for each row must follow the same as the first row:

```
<tr>
  <td>Introduction</td>
  <td>Egyptian hieroglyphs were a formal writing system
used by the ancient Egyptians which contained a combination
of logographic and alphabetic elements. Egyptians used
cursive hieroglyphs for religious literature on papyrus and
```

```
wood. Less formal variations of the script, called hieratic
and demotic, are technically not hieroglyphs.</td>
    <td> </td>
    <td>1</td>
    <td>Wikipedia.com</td>
</tr>
```

To pull in data you will need to add some additional content to the project. The first step is to add the following references to the Spry framework in the HEAD element of the page:

```
<script src="SpryAssets/SpryData.js" type="text/
javascript"></script>
    <script src="SpryAssets/SpryHTMLDataSet.js" type="text/
javascript"></script>
    <link href="SpryAssets/SpryMasterDetail.css"
rel="stylesheet" type="text/css" />
```

The three files allow you to connect to structured data. You will need to reference the history.html file in JavaScript within the HEAD element:

```
<script type="text/javascript">
    var ds1 = new Spry.Data.HTMLDataSet("history.
html", "history");
    ds1.setColumnType("Content", "html");
</script>
```

Figure P2.2 Adobe's Spry is used to pull in external data.

The first line of the script creates a new Spry dataset that has been labeled ds1. The dataset is pointing to a web page named history.html and is looking for a table with the ID "history".

The default formatting setting for Spry is plain text. The "content" column, however, contains HTML formatting that you want to bring into your app. The setColumnType allows you to specify a column and formatting.

There are two screens that will display Spry-generated data: the main History menu and History details screens, as shown in Figures P2.2 and P2.3.

The first screen, History menu, has a link from the main screen for the web app. For this reason, when you set up the History screen you must assign the ID "history" in the opening DIV element, as shown:

```
<div data-role="page" id="history" data-theme="e">
  <div data-role="header">
    <h1>History</h1>
  </div>
  <!-- /header -->
```

The HEADER element is a normal jQuery Mobile component. Things get a little different when you begin editing the "content" section.

The "content" begins as normal with a DIV element Data-role attribute identifying the section as "content".

Following that is a SPAN element. The SPAN element controls a section of HTML that will control how data is pulled into the page using the Spry framework. Notice that the spry:region identified is a reference to the ds1 dataset created using JavaScript in the HEAD element of the page.

The UL element defines a jQuery Mobile list:

```
<div data-role="content"> <span spry:region="ds1"
class="listClass">
    <ul id="quotes" selected="true" data-role="listview">
```

Following is a LIST ITEM (LI) element. Here is where you create your Spry template. The row uses the spry:repeat element to list all the data in the history.html file. A template reference labeled {LeadIn} places the content from the first column in the History.html document.

```
<li spry:repeat="ds1" spry:setrow="ds1" ><a
href="#details">{LeadIn}</a></li>
    </ul>
    </span><br>
    <br>
    <p><a href="#menu" data-role="button" >Back to Menu
</a></p>
    <br>
    <br>
    <br>
    </div>
</div>
```

The next step is to allow content selected in the LI element to appear in a screen labeled "Details". This leads to the third screen you need to create labeled Details.

As with the History screen, the Details screen starts as a normal jQuery Mobile screen, as shown in Figure P2.3.

```
<!-- Start of details page -->
<div data-role="page" id="details" data-
theme="e">
    <div data-role="header">
      <h1>History</h1>
    </div>
    <!-- /header -->
```

It is not until you reach the "content" section of the screen that you see a difference. As with the History screen you need to add a SPAN element which specifies that this is a detailregion for the dataset ds1:

```
<div data-role="content"> <span
spry:detailregion="ds1" class="DetailContainer">
```

Figure P2.3 The Details screen.

Following your specific reference you can then add references to columns of data you are pulling, as shown within the {} brackets:

```
<h2>{LeadIn}</h2>
<p class="DetailColumn">{Content}</p>
<br>
<p class="DetailColumn">Source: {Source}</p>
<br />
</span><br>
<br>
<p><a href="#menu" data-role="button" >Back to Menu</a>
</p>
<br>
<br>
<br>
</div>
<!-- /content -->
</div>
<!-- /page -->
```

Save your file.

At this point you can view your content within a mobile browser. The jQuery Mobile library will set the frame of the document. Content is pulled in dynamically with Spry. There are many other ways of pulling in dynamic data—Spry is just one example.

To publish your jQuery Mobile application you only need to upload the files to your website. It is as simple as that.

Summary

As you have seen in this project, jQuery Mobile allows you to build stunning web applications very quickly. Without a deep understanding of JavaScript or a programming language you can have an application running that looks and feels like a native app, albeit written in HTML.

Add dynamic data pulling techniques such as the Ajax-driven Spry and you can begin to create an app that can be easily managed. The data, visual elements, and business logic are all held in separate places.

The bottom line is you want to be able to deliver a rich, mobile-specific experience. This is what jQuery Mobile offers you today.

WORKING WITH jQTOUCH TO BUILD WEBSITES ON TOP OF jQUERY

Browser technologies are allowing you to bring rich applications into your web browser. In this chapter you will see how you can use the Open Source jQTouch Library to extend the functionality built into jQuery to build websites that run on your iOS and Android phones but look and interact as if they are native apps. You will learn how to create custom interfaces, screen flipping, and set themes using jQTouch.

Rapidly Building iPhone Apps without Learning Objective-C

Objective-C, the programming language used to create native apps for the iPhone, is not an easy language to learn. Although Steve Jobs espouses how easy it is to build an iPhone app (there are, after all, over 350,000), it is still not as easy as developing a website (there are billions of websites, in comparison). But this is all changing with tools such as jQTouch.

jQTouch is an open source plug-in for the jQuery library that allows you to very easily extend your website building skills to create solutions for the iPhone and Google's Android. You can get started using jQTouch by downloading it at *www.jqtouch.com/* as shown in Figure 3.1.

Something to note is that although jQTouch is built using HTML5 standards on top of the jQuery framework, it has not been optimized to run on all devices. For instance, response time on Windows Phone 7 has not been tested. jQTouch is optimized for Apple's iPhone (not the iPad) and will work well on Android phones (but not tablets).

Though it may seem highly selective, you do get some advantages that general-purpose platforms do not allow you to

Figure 3.1 The jQTouch website.

leverage. For instance, you can create a web app using jQTouch with a custom launch screen. This cannot be done with jQuery Mobile.

Take the time to review the features you will get in jQTouch before you download the jQTouch framework. In particular, notice how the extensions for jQTouch work. Leveraging just HTML5 skills you can add geolocation, automatic titles, and floating toolbars. No Objective-C is needed here.

Converting HTML into an iPhone App

The web browser built into the iPhone is one of the most advanced browsers on the market. Features such as CSS transitions and animation were part of the iPhone Mobile Safari web browser years before they reached the desktop. You can leverage advanced animation and JavaScript functions to create native, app-like solutions.

You will need to test the rest of the code we develop in this chapter either in Safari on your Mac or directly on an iOS device (iPhone, iPod Touch, or iPad). The code will run on all versions of iOS 3+ (I have not tested the code on iOS 2). Let me know if you have an iPhone OS 2 device and send me a tweet (@matthewadavid) or e-mail (matthewadavid@gmail.com). My gut is telling me that there are not too many of these devices out in the wild anymore.

To get you started you need to download the latest release of jQTouch. Point your web browser to *www.jqtouch.com/* and press the big, green Download button in the center of the screen. The code is stored in a Google Code Open Source project (*http://code.google.com/p/jqtouch/*), shown in Figure 3.2.

The jQTouch site has additional videos and tutorials you can check out. Also, check out Jonathan Stark's videos on YouTube (*www.youtube.com/user/jonathanstark*). These are great resources.

The jQTouch project comes packaged in a ZIP file you can expand. Pay attention to two main sections: the JavaScript files and the CSS/image files.

jQTouch is a jQuery plug-in. Much of the heavy lifting, when it comes to interactivity, is done for you.

Styling, animation, and formatting is accomplished with CSS and image files. You can update these files if you want, but in this chapter we are going to stick with the defaults.

Figure 3.2 The source code site for jQTouch.

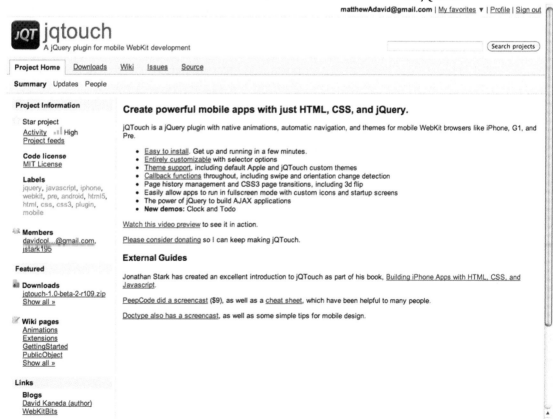

Building a Basic jQTouch Site

The goal of jQTouch is to allow you to create an iPhone-specific website very easily. To this end, all you really need is a little HTML, CSS, and some JavaScript knowledge to create your solutions. Let's start with a basic web page that is just using DIV and UL/LI elements.

Using your favorite text editor, such as Notepad++ (my favorite on the PC) or TextWrangler (my favorite on the Mac), create a new blank HTML page. Name the page template.html.

The first step is to declare that the document is HTML5 compliant. This is done by adding the DOCTYPE of HTML, as seen here:

```
<!doctype html>
```

The next step is to add some standard opening HTML tags and HEAD element content:

```
<html>
<head>
<meta charset="UTF-8" />
<title>Getting Started</title>
```

After the title, you will want to link to the CSS and JavaScript files used to design the document. You will see that the following CSS reference is pointing to a subfolder below the folder of the template. html document. Keeping your document references correct is very important. A mess-up here can lead to hours of bug hunting later.

You are linking to two CSS documents. The first is a generic document that contains information on page transitions, list presentation, and other visual elements. The second document points to a specific theme for the site. Here you are using the jqt theme. You can also use the "apple" folder for a theme (swap the jqt reference with apple) to give your web page an apple-esque look and feel.

```
<style type="text/css" media="screen">
@import "jqtouch/jqtouch.min.css";
</style>
<style type="text/css" media="screen">
@import "themes/jqt/theme.min.css";
</style>
```

Following the CSS reference, you will need to reference two JavaScript documents: the jQuery framework and jQTouch framework. Both are included with the downloaded files (as of writing this book, jQTouch has not been tested with jQuery 1.5.x but it should work).

```
<script src="jqtouch/jquery.1.3.2.min.js" type="text/
javascript" charset="utf-8"></script>
<script src="jqtouch/jqtouch.min.js" type="application/
x-javascript" charset="utf-8"></script>
```

Following the reference to the JavaScript files, you need to initialize the JavaScript onto the page. This is done by adding the following JavaScript:

```
<script type="text/javascript" charset="utf-8">
var jQT = new $.jQTouch({
});
</script>
```

After the references to the JavaScript frameworks you can close the HEAD and start the BODY elements.

```
</head>
<body>
```

Content presented as "page" on a screen is actually controlled by DIV elements in jQTouch. This is similar to jQuery Mobile. There are some syntactic differences between jQuery Mobile and jQTouch. For instance, jQuery Mobile uses custom attributes in the DIV elements for formatting whereas jQTouch uses class attributes as reference points for CSS.

Within the following DIV is a basic page structure:

```
<div id="home" class="current">
 <div class="toolbar">
  <h1>Template</h1>
 </div>
 <p>Welcome Screen</p>
</div>
```

The final step is to close the final HTML tags.

```
</body>
</html>
```

You will notice that the first DIV element has a class called "current". You can create additional pages using DIV elements. Adding the "current" class to one of them forces that page to be the default page displayed.

The second set of DIV elements leverages a class called "toolbar". The "toolbar" is a reference to a set of CSS files that add an iPhone-esque toolbar to the top of the screen.

All together it looks like this:

```
<!doctype html>
<html>
<head>
<meta charset="UTF-8" />
<title>Getting Started</title>
<style type="text/css" media="screen">
@import "jqtouch/jqtouch.min.css";
</style>
<style type="text/css" media="screen">
```

Figure 3.3 A basic template for your jQTouch applications.

```
@import "themes/jqt/theme.min.css";
</style>
<script src="jqtouch/jquery.1.3.2.min.js" type="text/
javascript" charset="utf-8"></script>
<script src="jqtouch/jqtouch.min.js" type="application/
x-javascript" charset="utf-8"></script>
<script type="text/javascript" charset="utf-8">
var jQT = new $.jQTouch({
});
</script>
</head>
<body>
<div id="home" class="current">
 <div class="toolbar">
  <h1>Template</h1>
 </div>
 <p>Welcome Screen</p>
</div>
</body>
</html>
```

Save your web page when you have added the links to the jQTouch files. Remember that when you first run this page in a web browser you are given a single page. Now when you run the web page, you are presented with a structured, app-like experience, as shown in Figure 3.3.

It is important to recognize that jQTouch is optimized for handheld devices. Unlike jQuery Mobile, which will scale the design to larger screens, jQTouch will only work for smaller screens. Your jQTouch solution will not work well on the iPad or other tablets.

Adding Two or More Pages

Creating the default template is a good place to start. Once you have it, you can open it, copy it, and start working on a second mobile app page. The next section will do this. Often, this is referred to as a boilerplate.

You can also add two or more screens as they appear on your phone. This is accomplished with additional DIV elements.

Let's start by taking the template we just created. Save the template with a new name, such as mulitpages.html. We'll begin by adding a default page in the main BODY section:

```
<div id="home" class="current">
 <div class="toolbar">
  <h1>Getting Started jQTouch</h1>
 </div>
 <a href="#pageTwo">Page Two</a>
</div>
```

Following the first set of DIV elements you can add a second set. Here you can see the reference for page two. You will see that the ID in the opening DIV is "pageTwo".

```
<div id="pageTwo">
 <div class="toolbar">
  <h1>Page Two</h1>
 </div>
</div>
```

The same process can be completed for page three:

```
<div id="pageThree">
 <div class="toolbar">
  <h1>Page Three</h1>
 </div>
</div>
```

At this point you can save your files and view them through either iOS or Android emulator. What you will see when you view the page is the first main page. You will not see the two new pages you have created.

To force the second page to be the first page to be presented inside of the mobile browser window you will need to change which DIV element has "class="current"". For instance, you can add the class "current" to the second page to make it the default page, as shown in Figure 3.4:

```
<div id="pageTwo" class="current">
 <div class="toolbar">
  <h1>Page Two</h1>
 </div>
 <p><a href="#home">back</a></p>
</div>
```

The way you can move around the site is to use HREF links. For instance, if the "pageTwo" DIV set is still the first loading page for the app, you can add a link to the home page with the following:

```
<div id="pageTwo" class="current">
 <div class="toolbar">
  <h1>Page Two</h1>
 </div>
 <p><a href="#home">Home</a></p>
</div>
```

All you have done is use the #home reference to an ANCHOR in your HTML. The ANCHOR is the ID name of the DIV element.

Figure 3.4 Changing the default start page for your website.

Following is the code from the three pages you have created with the addition of HREF links in each virtual page, giving your user the ability to link through different sections of the page:

```
<div id="home" class="current">
<div class="toolbar">
<h1>Getting Started</h1>
</div>
<a href="#pageTwo">Page Two</a>
<ul class="rounded">
    <li class="arrow"><a href="#pageTwo">Page Two</a>
<small class="counter">4</small></li>
    <li class="arrow"><a href="#pageThree">Page Three</a>
<small class="counter">8</small></li>
</ul>
</div>
<div id="pageTwo">
<div class="toolbar">
<h1>Page Two</h1>
</div>
<p><a href="#home">Home</a></p>
</div>
<div id="pageThree">
<div class="toolbar">
<h1>Page Three</h1>
</div>
<p><a href="#home">Home</a></p>
</div>
```

Save the page and preview in your mobile browser simulator, as shown in Figure 3.5.

Adding Lists

In the previous section you saw how to use a list to display data. Lists are effective tools you can leverage for your iPhone. This is largely due to the very limited space you have to work with on the screen. jQTouch gives you tools to easily add custom stylized lists.

You have three different types of lists in jQTouch: rounded, edge-to-edge, and metal. The effect of the three different types of list is very similar to the basic lists available in jQuery Mobile. Again, the difference, however, is that the jQTouch versions of the lists work great in iOS, are passable on Android, but have not been tested on any other system.

All three of the list types are enhancements of the standard UL and LI elements in HTML. The UL defines the type of list and the LI element leverages special classes to format the presentation of each list element.

Figure 3.5 A basic three-page site built with jQTouch.

Following is a basic example of a rounded list. You will see that the HTML is just an opening/closing UL element with list items, as shown in Figure 3.6:

```
<ul class="rounded">
 <li><a href="#link">Item One</a></li>
 <li><a href="#link">Item Two</a></li>
 <li><a href="#link">Item Three</a></li>
 <li><a href="#link">Item Four</a></li>
 <li><a href="#link">Item Five</a></li>
</ul>
```

The class reference to "rounded" changes the formatting. You can change the visual appearance of the list to an edge-to-edge style by changing the class reference (Figure 3.7):

```
<ul class="edgetoedge">
 <li><a href="#link">Item One</a></li>
 <li><a href="#link">Item Two</a></li>
 <li><a href="#link">Item Three</a></li>
 <li><a href="#link">Item Four</a></li>
 <li><a href="#link">Item Five</a></li>
</ul>
```

Finally, you can apply the metal style, again, by changing the class reference (Figure 3.8):

```
<ul class="metal">
 <li><a href="#link">Item One</a></li>
```

Figure 3.6 A "rounded" list.   Figure 3.7 An "edge-to-edge" list.   Figure 3.8 A "metal" list.

Figure 3.9 A "rounded" list with arrows.

Figure 3.10 Additional content added to the "rounded" list.

```
<li><a href="#link">Item Two</a></li>
<li><a href="#link">Item Three</a></li>
<li><a href="#link">Item Four</a></li>
<li><a href="#link">Item Five</a></li>
</ul>
```

Each list style also comes with its own set of special visual elements. For instance, the rounded list can have arrows added to each list item by simply adding a class to each list item that references the class name arrow, as shown in Figure 3.9:

```
<ul class="rounded">
<li class="arrow"><a href="#link">Item One</a></li>
<li class="arrow"><a href="#link">Item Two</a></li>
<li class="arrow"><a href="#link">Item Three</a></li>
<li class="arrow"><a href="#link">Item Four</a></li>
<li class="arrow"><a href="#link">Item Five</a></li>
</ul>
```

A second visual element you can add to rounded lists is a "counter" class reference to the right-hand side of the list element. Here you can see that each LI has a counter to the right-hand side within the SMALL element.

```
<ul class="rounded">
<li class="arrow"><a href="#link">Item One</a>
<small class="counter">1</small></li>
<li class="arrow"><a href="#link">Item Two</a>
<small class="counter">2</small></li>
<li class="arrow"><a href="#link">Item Three</a>
<small class="counter">3</small></li>
<li class="arrow"><a href="#link">Item Four</a>
<small class="counter">4</small></li>
<li class="arrow"><a href="#link">Item Five</a>
<small class="counter">5</small></li>
</ul>
```

Save this list to a web page and view inside your mobile browser, as shown in Figure 3.10.

Adding Buttons

There are three basic buttons you can use in jQTouch: two different buttons for the toolbar and one set of buttons you can add to the main screen.

It is becoming common to include a back button along the left-hand side of your toolbar to send you back to the previous screen. This can be done with jQTouch using HTML. The following adds a button in the toolbar, as shown in Figure 3.11.

```
<div id="home" class="current">
<div class="toolbar">
<a href="#" class="back">Back Btn</a>
```

```
    <h1>This is where you will add a title</h1>
  </div>
</div>
```

You will see in the previous HTML that the back button is a basic HREF link. The back button has an arrow shape that points to the left. Notice that the class is labeled "back" and that the button is before the H1 title. Placing the button before the title will force the button to be on the left-hand side of the title. If you want the button to be on the right-hand side of the title, then place the HTML after the H1.

In addition to the back button, you can also add a plain button. Here you can see the toolbar HTML content with a plain button:

```
<div id="home" class="current">
  <div class="toolbar">
   <h1>Buttons</h1>
   <a href="#" class="button">Plain Button</a>
  </div>
</div>
```

Figure 3.11 Buttons in jQTouch.

Again, as with the back button, the plain button is created using a HREF ANCHOR. The class, this time, is labeled "button" and the visual display does not have arrows. You will notice that I have placed the button after the label. Again, this is just a convention that is beginning to appear on many websites optimized for mobile devices.

The third button type is really a modification of a list type. Following is a list that comes with the class label of "individual". This creates a horizontal set of buttons. The following example shows two buttons.

```
    <h1>Using a List for a Button</h1>
      <ul class="individual">
        <li><a href="#;" target="_blank">Email</a></li>
        <li><a href="#" target="_blank">Button</a></li>
    </ul>
```

You can add up to five buttons.

Richer Form Elements

At some point you will need to add a form to your website. The form may be a "contact us" type of form, a "get more information" form, or even an entire shopping cart solution. Using forms within jQTouch is great. You do not need to use custom code, just plain HTML (jQTouch styles and formatting take care of the rest).

Here you can see that a standard HTML form has been added to the page. The one change to a standard form that you will notice is that each element in the form is wrapped in a list item (LI). This is just for formatting.

The form is wrapped in the FORM element within your HTML as shown here:

```
<div id="home" class="current">
 <div class="toolbar">
  <h1>Forms</h1>
 </div>
 <form>
```

Standard text input areas can leverage new HTML5 features such as placeholder text and input types. The following two are standard text and text areas, but you can use e-mail, phone, and other HTML5 input types to force the iPhone soft keyboard to change to the different types of default keyboard, as shown in Figure 3.12.

```
<ul class="edit rounded">
    <li><input type="text" name="name" placeholder="Text"
id="some_name" /></li>
    <li><input type="password" name="some_name"
value="qwerty" id="some_name" /></li>
    <li><textarea placeholder="Textarea" ></textarea></li>
```

A checkbox is a default yes/no or true/false feature in forms. You can see a SPAN element with the class label "toggle" to convert the checkbox element. Doing this creates the visual presentation of the checkbox to a slide for "on/off" options, as shown in Figure 3.13.

```
<li>Sample Toggle <span class="toggle"><input
type="checkbox" /></span></li>
```

A feature in iPhones is the spinning drum for lists. The following will create that same effect with the addition of allowing you to choose different categories, as shown in Figure 3.14:

Figure 3.12 Forms can be easily customized with jQTouch.

Figure 3.13 The toggle button is simply a checkbox—nice, huh?

Figure 3.14 The iOS drum roll options window.

```
<select id="itemList">
  <optgroup label="Vegetables">
    <option value ="Carrots">Carrots</option>
    <option value ="Cucumber">Cucumber</option>
  </optgroup>
  <optgroup label="Fruits">
    <option value ="Apple">Apple</option>
    <option value ="Orange">Orange</option>
  </optgroup>
</select>
  </li>
```

Checkboxes and Radio selectors can also be grouped together. Here you can see that standard HTML is used to organize the selectors by the name attribute.

```
<li><input type="checkbox" name="some_name"
value="Hello" id="some_name" title="V8 Engine Type" /></li>
    <li><input type="password" name="some_name" value="qwerty"
id="some_name"/></li>
    <li><input type="checkbox" name="some_name" value="Hello"
id="some_name" title="Eat Veggies" /></li>
    <li><input type="checkbox" name="some_name" value="Hello"
checked="checked" id="some_name" title="Each Fruit" /></li>
    <li><input type="radio" name="some_name" value="Hello"
id="some_name" title="Apples" /></li>
    <li><input type="radio" name="some_name" value="Hello"
id="some_name" title="Oranges" /></li>
    </ul>
    </form>
    </div>
```

As with standard HTML, you close your form with a </form> element. By leveraging HTML standards and jQTouch styles you can create beautiful forms with very little effort.

Adding a Floating Toolbar

The foundation for jQTouch is jQuery. A core feature of jQuery is the ability to extend the library with custom plug-ins. jQTouch can also be extended with plug-ins called "extensions." Three great plug-ins have been created by David Kaneda, called floaty, autotitles, and location.

Extensions are created with JavaScript. You will notice that they have the extension js, which indicates that they are JavaScript files.

Floaty is cool little tool that allows you to have a floating toolbar on your page. You can find the plug-in included with the jQTouch files with the folder names extensions.

Adding the floating toolbar does require some additional JavaScript, HTML, and CSS skills. Let's get started.

1. Open the Boilerplate template for jQTouch.
2. Save a copy of the web page and name it floating.html.

3. Open floating.html in your favorite text editor. A new JavaScript reference needs to be added to the other JavaScript files in the HEAD element of the page, as shown here:

```
<style type="text/css" media="screen">@import "jqtouch/
jqtouch.min.css";</style>
<style type="text/css" media="screen">@import "themes/
jqt/theme.min.css";</style>
<script src="jqtouch/jquery.1.3.2.min.js" type="text/
javascript" charset="utf-8"></script>
<script src="jqtouch/jqtouch.min.js" type="application/
x-javascript" charset="utf-8"></script>
<script src="extensions/jqt.floaty.js"
type="application/x-javascript" charset="utf-8"></script>
```

The final reference is to the jQTouch extension called floaty, named jqt.floaty.js. Notice that the file starts with the name jqt. This is a naming convention that lets you know that the file is an extension to the jQTouch framework.

The next step is to add some custom JavaScript. This code performs two functions: first the new plug-in is associated with the jQTouch framework; the second is to start the floating toolbar when the page loads.

```
<script type="text/javascript" charset="utf-8">
var jQT = new $.jQTouch({
});
$(function(){
$('.floatingToolbar).makeFloaty({
spacing: 20,
time: '1s'
});
});
</script>
```

This JavaScript has two settings you can control. The first is spacing, an instruction that states how far from the top of the screen the floating bar will appear. The second is time, an instruction for how long the floating bar animation will take to place the bar on the screen when you load the page.

After the JavaScript you will want to add a custom CSS class that will control how the toolbar will look on the screen:

```
<style type="text/css" media="screen">
.floatingToolbar {
-webkit-border-radius: 10px;
-webkit-box-shadow: rgba(0,0,0, .5) 0px 1px 1px;
width: 90%;
margin: 0 5%;
padding: 5px 10px;
background: rgba(255,255,255,.7);
color: #000;
}
</style>
```

You will notice these CSS settings control the same class in the JavaScript called floatingToolbar.

Each setting in the CSS is standard CSS3. You will notice for the background an RGBA setting is used to include an Alpha level (in this instance it is 70%). This is a relatively new color setting and the iPhone is one of the few systems to support it.

The final piece you need is the HTML to hold the floating toolbar. That can be done with the following:

```
<div class="floatingToolbar">
This is the floaty toolbar
</div>
```

Figure 3.15 shows the floating toolbar working.

Using Autotitles

The autotitle is a nice little script that will take your list name and create a web page for it. Using it is very easy. The setup is similar to the floating toolbar. The first thing you need to do is add a reference to the autotitle JavaScript file, as shown here:

Figure 3.15 The floating toolbar.

```
<style type="text/css" media="screen">@import "jqtouch/
jqtouch.min.css";</style>
<style type="text/css" media="screen">@import "themes/
jqt/theme.min.css";</style>
<script src="jqtouch/jquery.1.3.2.min.js" type="text/
javascript" charset="utf-8"></script>
<script src="jqtouch/jqtouch.min.js" type="application/
x-javascript" charset="utf-8"></script>
<script src="extensions/jqt.autotitles.js" type="application/
x-javascript" charset="utf-8"></script>
```

The next step is to add a list, as shown here:

```
<div id="page1">
      <div class="toolbar">
        <h1>Auto Titles</h1>
      </div>
      <ul class="edgetoedge">
        <li><a href="#page2">Quick Title One</a></li>
        <li><a href="#page2">Quick Title Two</a></li>
        <li><a href="#page2">Quick Title Three</a></li>
      </ul>
    </div>
```

The final step is to add a second page with a placeholder for the name in the toolbar. You will see that each of the links in the preceding list points to the same folder.

```
<div id="page2">
  <div class="toolbar">
    <a href="#" class="back">back</a>
    <h1>[Name]</h1>
  </div>
</div>
```

Figure 3.16 The autotitles extension.

Save your file and preview the page. Each time you select an item from the list, a new page will be generated with a new title, as shown in Figure 3.16.

Location Aware Solutions

The final plug-in leverages the geolocation features built into the phone to present the longitude and latitude of your current position.

This one will take a little more JavaScript.

As with the previous two plug-ins, you will need to reference the JavaScript files for this plug-in, as shown here:

```
<style type="text/css" media="screen">@import "jqtouch/
jqtouch.min.css";</style>
<style type="text/css" media="screen">@import "themes/
jqt/theme.min.css";</style>
<script src="jqtouch/jquery.1.3.2.min.js" type="text/
javascript" charset="utf-8"></script>
<script src="jqtouch/jqtouch.min.js" type="application/
x-javascript" charset="utf-8"></script>
<script src="extensions/jqt.location.js" type="application/
x-javascript" charset="utf-8"></script>
```

The next step is to add some additional JavaScript that allows for geolocation to work. The following script starts the new script:

```
<script type="text/javascript" charset="utf-8">
var jQT = new $.jQTouch({
});
```

The following function will display the content from the geolocation feature within your HTML where the info class is used:

```
$(function(){
function setDisplay(text) {
$('.info').empty().append(text)
}
```

The following if/else statement will create a string of text for the longitude and latitude.

```
var lookup = jQT.updateLocation(function(coords){
if (coords) {
setDisplay('Latitude: ' + coords.latitude + '<br />
Longitude: ' + coords.longitude);
} else {
setDisplay('Device not capable of geolocation.');
}
});
if (lookup) {
```

```
setDisplay('Looking up location&hellip;');
}
});
</script>
```

The final step is to add the HTML that will hold the geolocation coordinates. That can be accomplished with the following:

```
<div class="info"></div>
```

That's it. Save and test your code. You should now see the geolocation for your phone, as shown in Figure 3.17.

Creating Your Own Extensions

Extensions are a great way to add rich functionality within your jQTouch websites. Next I have pulled out the code from the autotitles extension so you can see how easy it is to create your own extensions.

The code starts by associating itself with the jQTouch framework:

```
(function($) {
    if ($.jQTouch)
    {
```

Figure 3.17 Geolocation in your iPhone.

The next step is to create a new function that will do the work. In this instance the function is named AutoTitles.

```
$.jQTouch.addExtension(function AutoTitles(jQT){
```

The first variable in the function is to look for content within any HTML (such as a DIV element) that uses both the toolbar class and the H1 element.

```
var titleSelector='.toolbar h1';
```

The second function creates a pseudo page from the list item.

```
$(function(){
$('body').bind('pageAnimationStart', function(e, data){
if (data.direction === 'in'){
var $title = $(titleSelector, $(e.target));
var $ref = $(e.target).data('referrer');
if ($title.length && $ref){
$title.html($ref.text());
}}})});
```

The final function sets the title of each page:

```
function setTitleSelector(ts){
titleSelector=ts;
}
return {
setTitleSelector: setTitleSelector
}});}
})(jQuery);
```

```
                                                                js  jqt.autotitles.js
 ◄   ►   js  jqt.autotitles.js  ⬍

 1  /*
 2
 3                    _/    _/_/    _/_/_/_/                           _/
 4                                                  _/                 _/
 5            _/  _/    _/_/    _/    _/    _/    _/    _/_/_/   _/_/_/
 6           _/  _/   _/    _/  _/    _/  _/    _/  _/    _/  _/    _/
 7          _/  _/_/_/   _/        _/    _/  _/    _/_/    _/_/    _/_/
 8          _/    _/
 9        _/
10
11      Created by David Kaneda <http://www.davidkaneda.com>
12      Documentation and issue tracking on Google Code <http://code.google.com/p/jqtouch/>
13
14      Special thanks to Jonathan Stark <http://jonathanstark.com/>
15      and pinch/zoom <http://www.pinchzoom.com/>
16
17      (c) 2009 by jQTouch project members.
18      See LICENSE.txt for license.
19
20  */
21
22  (function($) {
23      if ($.jQTouch)
24      {
25          $.jQTouch.addExtension(function AutoTitles(jQT){
26
27              var titleSelector='.toolbar h1';
28
29              $(function(){
30                  $('body').bind('pageAnimationStart', function(e, data){
31                      if (data.direction === 'in'){
32                          var $title = $(titleSelector, $(e.target));
33                          var $ref = $(e.target).data('referrer');
34                          if ($title.length && $ref){
35                              $title.html($ref.text());
36                          }
37                      }
38                  });
39              });
40
41              function setTitleSelector(ts){
42                  titleSelector=ts;
43              }
44
45              return {
46                  setTitleSelector: setTitleSelector
47              }
48
49          });
50      }
51  })(jQuery);
```

Figure 3.18 Editing JavaScript in Dashcode.

That's it. Not too bad. Check out how the code looks in Dashcode in Figure 3.18.

Both Jonathan Stark and David Kaneda have done a lot to enhance jQTouch over the last 18 months. Kudos to both of them.

Adding Animation

Animation is a big deal in iPhone applications. You can add fancy dissolves, cubic transitions, page flips, and more. The work that Apple has done in Mobile Safari allows the jQTouch project to easily expose these types of transitions for you.

The following example is a list of links that point to the same ANCHOR. Each link has a difference class reference to show how you can easily swap in and out different animation transitions.

```
<li><a href="#quote">Slide</a></li>
<li><a class="slideup" href="#quote">Slide Up</a></li>
<li><a class="dissolve" href="#quote">Dissolve</a></li>
<li><a class="fade" href="#quote">Fade</a></li>
<li><a class="flip" href="#quote">Flip</a></li>
<li><a class="pop" href="#quote">Pop</a></li>
<li><a class="swap" href="#quote">Swap</a></li>
<li><a class="cube" href="#quote">Cube</a></li>
```

Code that may require two or more class references can also be added. A good example where you may want to add animation and style formatting is with a button. The following code example shows that you can list two or more classes with each other:

```
class="button slideup"
```

The only thing you need to remember is to keep your references within quotes.

Some Little Extras

At this point you have the basic tools for creating a jQTouch website. There are, however, some nice little extras you can use that are specific for iOS devices.

The following function allows the animation to trigger correctly on the page.

```
<script type="text/javascript" charset="utf-8">
var jQT = new $.jQTouch({
});
$('#pageevents').
bind('pageAnimationStart', function(e, info){
$(this).find('.info').append('Started animating ' +
info.direction + '&hellip; ');
}).
bind('pageAnimationEnd', function(e, info){
$(this).find('.info').append(' finished animating ' +
info.direction + '.<br /><br />');
});
</script>
```

You can create a pseudo application with a custom launch page using jQTouch when the page has been saved to the main screen on the iPhone. The following settings link a default loading page, icon, icon style, and color to the status bar:

```
var jQT = new $.jQTouch({
icon: 'jqtouch.png',
addGlossToIcon: false,
startupScreen: 'jqt_startup.png',
statusBar: 'black',
```

It is important to note that the startup screen must be 480×320 pixels and that the icon must be 57×57 pixels. These settings work only for the iPhone; they will not work on the Android or other devices.

Summary

Using jQTouch is a fast way for you to convert a static web page into looking like a native iPhone or Android app. There is a lot of work currently being done by Jonathan Stark on jQTouch. This includes updating support for Android and modifying the tools for creating themes. The project is an Open Source solution. If you develop a new feature or fix a bug, don't forget to share your revelations with Jonathan. You might find your code merged into the main solution.

PROJECT: BUILDING A WEBSITE WITH jQTOUCH

The core to jQuery Mobile is jQuery, an open source framework that makes JavaScript just that little bit easier to work with. For mobile frameworks, though, jQuery Mobile was not the first kid on the block—that was jQTouch. Figure P3.1 illustrates the application you will build in this project.

You will see how you can leverage jQTouch to build a fully functional web application. The focus of the project is creating a tool that allows you to see where a fueling station is located.

What You Will Need

To get started with this project you will need to download the files from *www.visualizetheweb.com*. The files for this project are contained in a ZIP file that you can extract on your desktop.

All you need to build the project are the following project files:
- Index.html
- map.html
- Images folder (with one image)
- jQTouch documents (containing two JavaScripts and one CSS document)

Setting Up Your jQTouch Project

Let's get down to business and step through the main document for this project. Most of your work will be completed in the main index.html web page.

The app is an HTML5 document and starts as a standard HTML5 web page:

```
<html>
<head>
<title>Gas2GO!</title>
```

Figure P3.1 jQTouch used to format the web pages.

The following three META elements are specific to Apple's iPhone. Unlike jQuery Mobile, jQTouch specifically targets first iPhone, then Android, and finally BlackBerry. It does not attempt to run on all devices.

```
<meta name="viewport" content="width=device-
width; initial-scale=1.0; maximum-scale=1.0; user-
scalable=0;" />
    <meta name="apple-mobile-web-app-capable"
content="yes" />
    <meta names="apple-mobile-web-app-status-bar-
style" content="black-translucent" />
```

The following points to the core jQTouch Cascading Style Sheet document and then a specific theme.

```
<link type="text/css" rel="stylesheet"
media="screen" href="jqtouch/jqtouch.css">
    <link type="text/css" rel="stylesheet"
media="screen" href="themes/jqt/theme.css">
```

The following two JavaScript files are the core jQuery library and the jQTouch library:

```
<script type="text/javascript" src="jqtouch/
jquery-1.4.2.min.js"></script>
    <script type="text/javascript" src="jqtouch/
jqtouch.js"></script>
```

As with any web page, you can add custom JavaScript. Here, the following script extends the functionality of the core jQTouch framework. These classes allow you to set a default icon, startup screen logo, and status bar color:

```
<script type="text/javascript" charset="utf-8">
var jQT = new $.jQTouch({
icon: 'logo.png',
addGlossToIcon: false,
startupScreen: 'jqt_startup.png',
statusBar: 'black',
```

It is useful to have some of the images used frequently in the application preloaded. The following function allows you to do just this:

```
preloadImages: [
'../../themes/jqt/img/back_button.png',
'../../themes/jqt/img/back_button_clicked.png',
'../../themes/jqt/img/button_clicked.png',
'../../themes/jqt/img/grayButton.png',
'../../themes/jqt/img/whiteButton.png',
'../../themes/jqt/img/loading.gif'
]
});
```

The following is a page animation callback event:

```
$('#pageevents').
bind('pageAnimationStart', function(e, info){
$(this).find('.info').append('Started animating ' +
info.direction + '&hellip; ');
}).
bind('pageAnimationEnd', function(e, info){
$(this).find('.info').append(' finished animating ' +
info.direction + '.<br /><br />');
});
```

All page animations end with an Ajax callback event as shown:

```
$('#callback').bind('pageAnimationEnd', function
(e, info){
if (!$(this).data('loaded')) {
$(this).append($('<div>Loading</div>').
load('ajax.html .info', function() {
$(this).parent().data('loaded', true);
})));
}
});
// Orientation callback event
$('body').bind('turn', function(e, data){
$('#orient').html('Orientation: ' + data.
orientation);
});
});
</script>
```

Additional Cascading Style Classes extend the core properties of the main jQTouch CSS document. The following extends functionality of the main "header" section:

```
<style type="text/css">
div.wrapper { width: 940px; margin: 0 auto; padding:
0 30px 36px; position: relative; }
div#header { background: #f5f5f5; height: 72px; border-
bottom: 1px solid #eee; margin: 0; }
div#header h4 { float: left; position: absolute; top:
24px; left: 145px; border-left: 1px solid #ddd; padding-
left: 14px; }
div#header h4 small { font-size: 14px; font-weight:
normal; }
div#header h4 a, div#header h4 a:visited { font-weight:
normal; }
div.page-header { padding: 0 0 8px; margin: 18px 0;
border-bottom: 1px solid #ddd; }
div.page-header h1 { padding: 0; margin: 0; font-size:
24px; line-height: 27px; letter-spacing: 0; }
```

The "awesome" class is extended here:

```
.awesome, .awesome:visited {background: #222 url(/
images/alert-overlay.png) repeat-x; display: inline-block;
padding: 5px 10px 6px; color: #fff; text-decoration:
none;-moz-border-radius: 5px; -webkit-border-radius:
5px;-moz-box-shadow: 0 1px 3px rgba(0,0,0,0.5);-
webkit-box-shadow: 0 1px 3px rgba(0,0,0,0.5);text-
shadow: 0 -1px 1px rgba(0,0,0,0.25);border-bottom:
1px solid rgba(0,0,0,0.25);position: relative;cursor:
pointer;width:100%;}
    .awesome:hover{ background-color: #111; color: #fff; }
    .awesome:active{ top: 1px; }
    .small.awesome, .small.awesome:visited { font-size:
11px;}
    .awesome, .awesome:visited,
    .medium.awesome, .medium.awesome:visited { font-size:
13px; font-weight: bold; line-height: 1; text-shadow:
0 -1px 1px rgba(0,0,0,0.25); }
    .large.awesome, .large.awesome:visited { font-size:
14px; padding: 8px 14px 9px; }
    .green.awesome, .green.awesome:visited{ background-
color: #91bd09; }
    .green.awesome:hover{ background-color: #749a02; }
    .blue.awesome, .blue.awesome:visited{ background-color:
#2daebf; }
    .blue.awesome:hover{ background-color: #007d9a; }
    .red.awesome, .red.awesome:visited{ background-color:
#e33100; }
    .red.awesome:hover{ background-color: #872300; }
    .magenta.awesome, .magenta.awesome:visited{ background-
color: #a9014b; }
    .magenta.awesome:hover{ background-color: #630030; }
    .orange.awesome, .orange.awesome:visited{ background-
color: #ff5c00; }
    .orange.awesome:hover{ background-color: #d45500; }
    .yellow.awesome, .yellow.awesome:visited{ background-
color: #ffb515; }
    .yellow.awesome:hover{ background-color: #fc9200; }
</style>
</head>
```

The next step is to add the first screen that will show on the page. All the screens are managed using DIV elements. As with jQuery Mobile, all the screens are loaded and managed with one web page, and are shown as "screens" on the iPhone.

The following block of HTML is the main home screen that loads by default when the application runs on a website. There are two main sections to the page: the toolbar and main content:

```
<div id="home">
<div class="toolbar">
<h1>Gas2GO</h1>
```

```
    <a class="button flip" href="#settings">My Account
</a>
    </div>
    <ul class="plastic">
    <li class="arrow"><a href="#dates">Fuel Purchases</a>
</li>
    <li class="arrow"><a href="#sos">SOS</a></li>
    <li class="arrow"><a href="map.html" target="_
webapp">Find Fuel</a></li>
    <li class="arrow"><a href="#about">About</a></li>
    </ul>
    </div>
```

The structure of this screen can be seen in other screens in the application as shown:

```
    <div id="nearest1">
    <div class="toolbar">
    <h1>Station #1288</h1>
    <a class="button back" href="#">Back</a>
    </div>
    <ul class="rounded">
    <p> </p>
    <span class="headlineRed">Station is Closed
    </span>
    <p> </p>
    <button class="large yellow awesome" style="margin-
left:auto;margin-right:auto;">
    <h1><a href="tel:5555555555">Call Station #1288</a>
</h1>
    </button>
    <p> </p>
    <p><span style="color: #FFF;">
    Time to station: 8 mins<br>
    Amount of Fuel At Station: 15 liters<br>
    </span></p>
    </ul>
    </div>
```

You can step through most of the code in the web page and you will see that the app follows the same structure in managing content in a screen.

One screen that deserves additional attention is the settings screen. The settings screen is different for a simple reason: it contains a form.

The setup for the page is very similar to a normal screen, as follows:

```
    <div id="settings">
    <div class="toolbar">
    <h1>Settings</h1>
    <a class="button back" href="#">Back</a>
    </div>
```

Things get slightly different when you reach the form itself. For the most part, the form is a standard HTML form, as shown in Figure P3.2. What is different is the use of HTML5 Form attributes to control how data is viewed and entered in each FORM element. You can see that the Placeholder attribute is used extensively.

```
<form method="post">
<h1>Credit Card</h1>
<ul class="rounded">
   <li><input placeholder="Credit Card Number"
type="text" name="age" id="age" /></li>
   <li><input placeholder="Name on Card Number"
type="text" name="age" id="age" /></li>
   <li><input placeholder="Credit Card Number"
type="text" name="age" id="age" /></li>
   <li><input placeholder="Amount" type="text"
name="weight" id="weight" /></li>
   <li><input type="submit" class="submit"
name="action" value="Save Changes" /></li>
   </ul>
   </form>
   </div>
```

Save the files and preview them on an iPhone. You are presented with a solution that looks and feels very much like a native application, but is running in a web page.

Figure P3.2 A form built with jQTouch.

Summary

On the whole, jQTouch is a solid framework for iPhones. It is easy to edit and control. The framework does lose some traction for websites that require support for a broader range of mobile devices. But it makes for a good base to get you started.

USING SENCHA TOUCH TO BUILD A MOBILE WEBSITE

Up to this point you have been using a mixture of HTML, CSS, and JavaScript to construct your mobile websites. In this section we are going to use Sencha's (*www.sencha.com*) Touch framework to construct your mobile websites.

The significant difference between Sencha Touch and jQuery Mobile and HTML5 development is the heavy use of JavaScript to programmatically construct your pages. The negative to this is that you will need to be comfortable using JavaScript; the plus is that you can do some crazy cool things.

At this point I do need to point out one specific difference between Sencha Touch and frameworks such as jQuery Mobile. jQuery Mobile seeks to work on a broad range of mobile devices; in contrast Sencha Touch targets specific devices, namely iOS, Android 2.1+, and BlackBerry 6 devices, as shown in Figure 4.1. The rationale for this is simple: the majority of next generation smart phones run on iOS, Android, or BlackBerry.

Getting Started with Sencha Touch

Sencha Touch is a free solution, but with a more complex licensing program than jQuery Mobile. The licensing that will likely interest you most is the GNU GPL Open Source license. Essentially, what this means is that any changes you make to the core library can be shared with other users of the code base; if, however, you want to keep your enhancements proprietary then contact Sencha about purchasing a Commercial Software License. I can't imagine there are too many calls for the paid version of the software.

The bottom line is that the Sencha Touch framework is free for most of us. And that is great news.

Sencha Touch can be downloaded from the Sencha website. Go to *www.sencha.com/products/touch/*, as shown in Figure 4.2.

The Sencha Touch framework is contained within a large ZIP file. Open the ZIP file on your computer and extract the content.

As with all popular mobile frameworks there are three main parts to the Sencha Touch framework: a JavaScript file, CSS, and

Figure 4.1 The Sencha Touch website shows its software running on iPhone, Android, and BlackBerry.

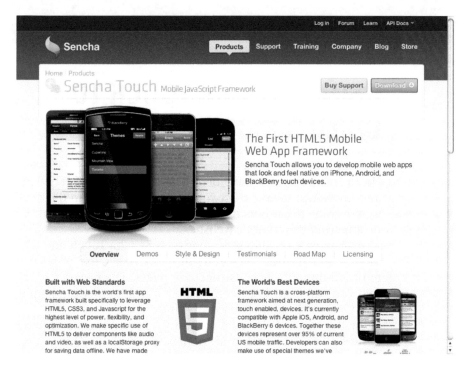

Figure 4.2 Where to go to download the files.

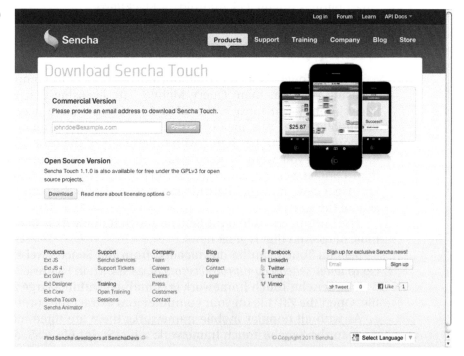

HTML5. There are some big differences, however. To begin with, Sencha places a much heavier focus on JavaScript to describe the structure of the content over HTML5 elements. The second is an extension of CSS3 named SASS.

So why is there a heavy reliance on JavaScript? 'Tis a good question, young squire. Fundamentally it comes down to a reflection of Sencha's history with JavaScript. Sencha Touch has its foundation based on traditional desktop JavaScript frameworks such as Sencha's Ext JS. So, you work with what you know. There is also a second advantage to using JavaScript over HTML: device type. We know that an ever-increasing number of devices are vying for your attention: iPhones, Android Phones, iPad, PlayBooks, the list goes on and on. Leveraging JavaScript, Sencha is able to extend Sencha Touch to easily adapt to tablet devices. Later in the series you will see how you can leverage the skills you learn in this chapter to build out tablet interfaces using the exact same JavaScript. It is pretty cool stuff.

The document that does all the heavy lifting in Sencha Touch is named sencha-touch.js. You can open sencha-touch.js to view the code. It will be difficult to read because the code has been minimized to reduce the size of the file. Here is what the first function looks like:

```
{Ext={}}Ext.apply=(function(){for(var a in {valueOf:1})
{return function(c,b,e){if(e){Ext.apply(c,e)}if(c&&b&&typeof
b==="object"){for(var d in b){c[d]=b[d]}}return c}}return
function(c,b,e){if(e){Ext.apply(c,e)}if(c&&b&&typeof
b==="object"){for(var d in b){c[d]=b[d]}if(b.toString!==Object.
prototype.toString){c.toString=b.toString}if(b.valueOf!
==Object.prototype.valueOf){c.valueOf=b.valueOf}}return c}})();
```

To help you understand the inner workings of Sencha Touch, you can also view the JavaScript in a debug version (sencha-touch-debug. js). The same line just shown looks like this in debug:

```
Ext.apply = (function() {
    for(var key in {valueOf:1}) {
      return function(object, config, defaults) {
            if (defaults) {
          Ext.apply(object, defaults);
        }
        if (object && config && typeof config == 'object') {
          for (var key in config) {
            object[key] = config[key];
          }
        }
        return object;
    };
  }
})();
```

Yes, that is much easier to read. But, before we get too carried away with ourselves, let's get our default Sencha Touch template completed.

Creating Your First Sencha Touch Page

You will need to get your favorite text editor out for working with Sencha Touch for the heavy lifting. We also have some graphics to develop, so crank up GIMP, Photoshop, Fireworks, or your favorite graphics editor.

If you have not already done so, download Sencha Touch and expand the files. You will see a *lot* of folders with subfolders. What you are looking for are:

*   A folder called "resource"
*   A file called Sencha-touch.js

These are the files you need to start your template. Let's go ahead and add some more.

Start by creating a new HTML5 page. Let's call it boilerplate. html. Unlike jQuery Mobile and jQTouch, the displayed content for your site will not be in HTML but will be controlled using JavaScript. With that said you do need to link to the JavaScript files and CSS files that control the presentation. The following will form the base for your Sencha Touch web app:

```
<!DOCTYPE html>
<html>
<head>
<meta charset="utf-8">
<title>Boilerplate</title>
<!--Sencha Touch CSS-->
<link rel="stylesheet" href="resources/css/sencha-touch.css" type="text/css">
<!--Sencha Touch CSS-->
<script type="text/javascript" src="sencha-touch.js">
</script>
</head>
<body></body>
</html>
```

The code itself is standard HTML5. The opening DOCTYPE is the HTML5 document type. At line seven is a reference to the default Sencha Touch CSS document. Line nine refers to the core minimized Sencha Touch JavaScript document.

At this point if you run your web page inside of a mobile phone you will not see anything. The CSS and JavaScript files are the foundation you need for your apps. To get anything working with Sencha Touch you need to add an additional JavaScript file. To keep things easy to manage, let's add the JavaScript you will use to power your app with a second JS file. Name the file boilerplate.js and add the following link after the sencha-touch.js file reference in your boilerplate.html page:

```
<script type="text/javascript" src="boilerplate.js">
</script>
```

The file named boilerplate.js forms the base of your Sencha Touch application. There are two main parts of the app file: settings and presentation.

Each Sencha Touch web app you create can inherit native-app-like settings. For instance, the following four settings allow a Sencha Touch app that is saved to the home screen to have its own icon, iPhone startup screen, and iPad startup screen:

```
Ext.setup({
  icon: 'icon.png',
  glossOnIcon: false,
  tabletStartupScreen: 'tablet_startup.png',
  phoneStartupScreen: 'phone_startup.png',
});
```

Stepping through each line, the first line initializes the setup settings. The second line links to a PNG file called icon.png. iOS requires you provide a 57×57 pixel file labeled icon to be the icon on the home screen of your iPhone.

By default, all icons on iOS devices have a glossy interface. Changing the setting for glossOnIcon to false removes Apple's default visual effect.

The iPad can use an image while your app is starting up. The image is 1024×768 pixels. iPhone and iPod Touch devices will use an image while your app is starting up. The image is 480×360 pixels.

At this point we still do not have anything visual to display. Append the following JavaScript to the bottom of your boilerplate.js file.

```
onReady. function() {
    new Ext.TabPanel({
       fullscreen: true,
       type: 'dark',
       items: [{
           title: 'Tab 1',
           html: '<p>This is a place for HTML</p> <p>feel
free to add your content</p>',
           cls: 'card1'
       }]
    });
}
```

Figure 4.3 Your first Sencha Touch web page.

The onReady function controls the content that will be presented on the screen. The DOM for the mobile browser fires the onReady code when it is fully loaded.

This section contains settings for the Sencha Touch TabPanel. In this instance you only have one tab on the screen. We'll cover the TabPanel in more detail later.

All together, your boilerplate.js file should look like the following, as shown in Figure 4.3:

```
Ext.setup({
    icon: 'icon.png',
    glossOnIcon: false,
    tabletStartupScreen: 'tablet_startup.png',
    phoneStartupScreen: 'phone_startup.png',
    onReady: function() {
        new Ext.TabPanel({
            fullscreen: true,
            type: 'dark',
            items: [{
                title: 'Tab 1',
                html: '<p>This is a place for HTML</p>
<p>feel free to add your content</p>',
                cls: 'card1'
            }]
        });
    }
});
```

You can now run the files in your mobile browser and present them as a web page with one tab on it.

The next section examines the different UI tools Sencha Touch provides.

Working with User Interface Elements in Sencha Touch

As with all the frameworks we cover, Sencha Touch comes with a set of iOS/Android app-like UI tools you can add to your web apps. The collection is very extensive and includes the following:

- Buttons
- Forms
- Lists
- Toolbars
- Carousel and tabs
- Video

Each of these elements are constructed with JavaScript and formatted with CSS. You can use the default CSS settings or, when you are comfortable working with the code base, even go into the CSS file to make your own modifications.

The key to remember is that each feature is just JavaScript and CSS, which means you can extend them with your own script.

Adding Buttons to a Page

There are dozens of color schemes and styles for buttons in Sencha Touch. What you will find is that they are all structured with simple parameter settings. For instance, the following will add a standard button:

```
items: [
        { text:button 'Standard' },
]
```

The button itself is described within the square brackets as an item. You have a setting called text. The result is a gray, square button with the word Standard written on it.

A rounded button can be created by adding the parameter ui: 'round' as shown here:

```
items: [
    { ui: 'round', text: 'Round' }
]
```

Buttons can also be set to perform specific functions. For instance, a default button can be used to trigger a command, or to cancel an action. The following two buttons will confirm and decline an action. The ui attribute defines both look and functionality.

```
items: [
        { ui: 'decline-round', text: 'No Thank You' }
        ]
   }, {
     items: [
        { ui: 'confirm', text: 'Approve' },
]
```

There are over 50 different styles of buttons you can use in Sencha Touch. And, of course, you can use CSS to create your own custom styles, as shown in Figure 4.4.

Controlling Forms In Sencha Touch

Sencha provides you with a complete set of form controls, as shown in Figure 4.5. As with buttons, you will see that the form controls are presented as items that can be configured with property values.

A form is comprised of a fieldset region wrapped in square brackets, as shown:

```
items: [{
        xtype: 'fieldset',
        title: 'Online Information',
        instructions: 'Please enter the information above.',
        defaults: {
```

Figure 4.4 Different buttons in the Sencha Touch framework.

Figure 4.5 Sencha Touch comes with a broad range of form controls.

```
          //labelAlign: 'right'
          labelWidth: '25%'
        },
  }]
```

The second line in the example declares that xtype is a form. The third and fourth line are titles and descriptions you can add.

Of course, this form does not have any content. You can add form fields and controls before the closing }] at the end in the last line.

There are several form controls you can add including:

- Text field
- Text area
- Password
- Email
- URL field
- Checkbox
- Date picker
- Selection
- Hidden

Each field is controlled in a very similar way: you have an xtype describing the field and then a set of parameters that add additional information. For instance, this is how you describe a text field:

```
items: [{
          xtype: 'textfield',
          name: 'nameID',
          'Name',
          placeHolder: 'Matthew David',
          autoCapitalize : true,
          required: true,
        },
```

The xtype 'textfield' informs Sencha Touch to reformat the item as a text field. The name property is an ID you can use to reference the field. The label property places a label to the left-hand side of the field.

Text can be placed into the form field as placeholder text. In this instance I have added my name (you can add your own name).

The autoCapitalize property allows for auto-capitalization of the first letter of each word. This is a Boolean true or false setting. If you set the field to being required then a star will be placed alongside the label.

The Text field is the most basic form field in the Sencha Touch framework. There are, however, four other fields that are very similar: Text area, Password, URL, and Email.

At the basic level, each of these four fields are just different enhancements of the Text field but with additional special properties. Below is a breakdown of the four field types as you define them in Sencha Touch:

```
{
        xtype: 'passwordfield',
        name: 'password',
        label: 'Password',
        useClearIcon: true
    }, {
        xtype: 'emailfield',
        name: 'email',
        label: 'Email',
        placeHolder: "matthewadavid@gmail.com"',
        useClearIcon: true
    }, {
        xtype: 'urlfield',
        name: 'url',
        label: 'Url',
        placeHolder: 'http://focalpress.com',
        useClearIcon: true
    }, {
        xtype: 'textareafield',
        name: 'bio',
        label: 'Bio'
    }]
}
```

Figure 4.6 The password field extends the functionality of the text field.

Sencha Touch is leveraging new HTML5 features in forms to control how you interact with passwords or e-mail fields. For instance, when you select the Password field type your characters are changed to bullets as you type in the password, as shown in Figure 4.6. Nothing special here (this has been the case with password fields for years), but it starts getting cool with the e-mail field.

The e-mail field modifies the onscreen keyboard to one specifically for e-mail characters. The @ symbol is prominently displayed on the new keyboard, as shown in Figure 4.7.

The URL field is similar in that you have fast access to special keys such as one with the extension .com as shown in Figure 4.8.

Through extending the base text field, Sencha Touch allows you to easily leverage complex HTML5 features supported in iOS devices and Android 2.3+.

The good news is that support for complex form features does not stop with text fields. The checkbox is another field you can add to your forms to solicit a simple true/false, or Boolean, response. To use the checkbox you leverage the xtype named checkboxfield, as shown:

```
{   xtype: 'checkboxfield',
    name: 'doYouLikeRain',
    label: 'Do you like rain?'
}
```

Figure 4.7 The e-mail text field has a custom keyboard.

Figure 4.8 The URL text field has a custom keyboard.

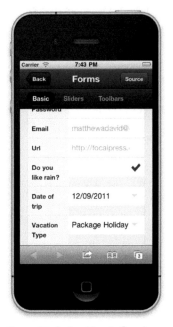

Figure 4.9 A checkbox in Sencha Touch is a big check mark.

Figure 4.10 The scrolling barrel is the Sencha Touch alternative to a drop down list.

As you can see, the checkbox has only a few parameters you need to set. Once you have them set you will see on your Android or iPhone that you can answer the question with a check mark, as shown in Figure 4.9.

Dates can also be controlled with the datepickerfield.

```
{
    xtype: 'datepickerfield',
    name: 'dateOfTrip',
    label: 'Date of trip',
    picker: { yearFrom: 2010 }
}
```

Selecting a date from the datepickerfield will bring up a screen that will allow you to select year/month/day from a spinning tumbler. All of this is completed with HTML.

A similar control to the datepickerfield is the selectfield form control. The objective of the selectfield control is to allow you to choose two or more options from a pop-up tumbler screen. The selectfield is comprised of two parts: the selectfield and the options that will appear on the screen, as shown in Figure 4.10.

Below selectfield you can choose from different types of vacation trip:

```
{
    xtype: 'selectfield',
    name: 'vacation',
    label: 'Vacation Type',
    options: [{
    text: 'Package Holiday',
    value: 'package'
}, {
    text: 'RV',
    value: 'rv'
}, {
    text: 'Hotel',
    value: 'hotel'
}, {
    text: 'Camping',
    value: 'camping'
}, {
    text: 'Youth Hostel',
    value: 'youthHostel'
}]
}
```

Figure 4.11 The selectfield option gives you several options to choose from.

Each item you can select from the onscreen display has two properties: text and value. The text value is the screen display for the form. The value is the data that will be sent to your database/server, as shown in Figure 4.11.

Similar to the selectfield xtype is the fieldset xtype for creating a group of radio buttons. Yep, this is very much like creating a group of radio buttons on a web page where the customer can select only one option.

The setup for the fieldset is very similar to the selectfield: you have a control that manages the items. Here is an example of fieldset group:

```
{
    xtype: 'fieldset',
    title: 'Travel Options',
    defaults: {
      xtype: 'radiofield',
      labelWidth: '35%'
    },
    items: [{
      name: 'travel',
      value: 'car',
      label: 'Car'
    }, {
      name: 'travel',
      label: 'Bus',
      value: 'bus'
    }, {
```

```
      name: 'travel',
      label: 'Camper',
      value: 'Camper'
    }, {
      name: 'travel',
      label: 'RV',
      value: 'rv'
    }, {
      name: 'travel',
      label: 'Plane',
      value: 'plane'
  }]
```

You will see that the items you can select are very similar to the selectfield. The big difference, however, is that each item has a name property. Each item has the same value in the name property. Keeping the value the same tells Sencha Touch that these values are in the same group. The resulting action is that the user can select only one option.

The final action for any form is to add a Submit button. This is where you use the Sencha Touch UI buttons covered earlier.

Controlling Data with Lists Using Sencha Touch

Sencha Touch comes with three list types: basic, grouped, and disclosure. The three lists scroll up and down with iOS-like momentum giving you an app-like feel to your page.

The setup for each of the lists is very similar. You have three key elements: defining the values you will be presenting, the data itself, and the list control. In many ways, it is not too different from the selectfield and fieldset form controls. This is why I like Sencha Touch—each control becomes more complex by enhancing existing design patterns and thereby reducing your learning curve. Nice, huh?

To demonstrate how lists work in Sencha Touch, we'll use an example: to display a list of campgrounds. The list itself is a local array, but you can use XML or JSON to populate the list, too.

Start by instructing Sencha Touch that you are creating a new data model, and identifying the fields you will be accessing within that model. The following three lines provide the instruction:

```
Ext.regModel('Camping', {
    fields: ['campsiteName', 'locationState']
});
```

The first line defines the name of the model. In this instance, we are calling it 'Camping'. The second line defines the fields you will use, in this case 'campsiteName' and 'locationState'.

The next step is to add the array you will use for your data source:

```
demos.ListStore = new Ext.data.Store({
  model: 'Camping',
  sorters: 'campsiteName',
  getGroupString : function(record) {
      return record.get('campsiteName')[0];
  },
  data: [
{campsiteName: 'Bridge Bay', locationState: 'CA'},
{campsiteName: 'Canyon', locationState: 'CO'},
{campsiteName: 'Fishing Bridge', locationState: 'CO'},
{campsiteName: 'Grant Village', locationState: 'ND'},
{campsiteName: 'Lewis Lake', locationState: 'SD'},
{campsiteName: 'Madison', locationState: 'WI'},
{campsiteName: 'Mammoth', locationState: 'CA'},
{campsiteName: 'Norris', locationState: 'MA'},
{campsiteName: 'Pebble Creek', locationState: 'MA'},
{campsiteName: 'Door County', locationState: 'MA'},
{campsiteName: 'Slough Creek', locationState: 'MA'},
{campsiteName: 'Tower', locationState: 'MA'},
{campsiteName: 'Arches', locationState: 'MA'},
{campsiteName: 'Canyon Lands', locationState: 'MA'},
{campsiteName: 'Rushmore', locationState: 'MA'},
  ]
});
```

The first line assigns a name to the new array, or data store. By giving the data store a name you can then tie it to other controls. We will do that in a moment.

The second line identifies the model name and links it with the model defined in the previous section.

The data itself is a list of value pairs: a name and a value. In this instance the data names are campsiteName and locationState. With this information you can now create the visual elements of the list.

The basic list forms the foundation for the three different types of list. Below is a breakdown of a basic list:

```
items: [{
    title: 'Basic',
    layout: Ext.is.Phone ? 'fit' : {
        type: 'vbox',
        align: 'center',
        pack: 'center'
    },
    cls: 'demo-list',
    items: [{
        width: Ext.is.Phone ? undefined : 300,
        height: 500,
```

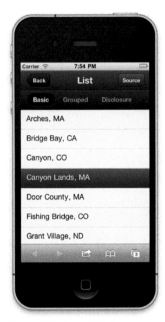

Figure 4.12 A basic list.

```
        xtype: 'list',
        store: demos.ListStore,
        itemTpl: '<div class="Camping"><strong>{campsit
eName}</strong>, {locationState}</div>'
        }]
    }
```

The list is in two main parts: the first section defines how the list will look on the screen and the second section, from line 8, controls the data.

The important properties are xtype, store, and itemTpl. The xtype defines that this is a list to be displayed. The store points to the array you created.

The itemTpl is a template you use to control how the data is displayed on the screen. In this example you are using some simple HTML with placeholders for the data.

You can now save the file and view it inside your mobile browser, as shown in Figure 4.12. Voilà! A basic list.

Lists can be more complicated by adding additional Sencha Touch list properties. For instance, the following is a basic list that now groups all the items by letter.

```
    {
        title: 'Grouped',
        layout: Ext.is.Phone ? 'fit' : {
            type: 'vbox',
            align: 'center',
            pack: 'center'
        },
        cls: 'demo-list',
        items: [{
    width: Ext.is.Phone ? undefined : 300,
    height: 500,
    xtype: 'list',
    store: demos.ListStore,
    itemTpl: '<div class="Camping"><strong>{campsiteName}</
strong> {locationState}</div>',
            grouped: true,
            indexBar: true
        }]
    }
```

Figure 4.13 A most complex list.

The grouping is controlled with the inclusion of a property called grouped. Setting this value to true will group everything together.

An additional property, indexBar, will add an alphabetical bar along the right-hand side of the screen, allowing you to quickly tap a letter, as shown in Figure 4.13. That's it. You have created a second type of list by merely enhancing the existing basic list.

Finally, you can add even more complexity. In the following example, as shown in Figure 4.14, you can select an item in the list, tap it, and present a pop-up box with more information:

```
{
    title: 'Disclosure',
    layout: Ext.is.Phone ? 'fit' : {
        type: 'vbox',
        align: 'center',
        pack: 'center'
    },
    cls: 'demo-list',
    items: [{
        width: Ext.is.Phone ? undefined : 300,
        height: Ext.is.Phone ? undefined : 500,
        xtype: 'list',
        onItemDisclosure: function(record, btn, index) {
            Ext.Msg.alert('Tap', 'Disclose more info for '
+ record.get('campsiteName'), Ext.emptyFn);
        },
        store: demos.ListStore, //getRange(0, 9),
        itemTpl: '<div class="Camping"><strong>{campsite
Name}</strong> {locationState}</div>'
    }]
}
```

Figure 4.14 An even more complex list.

As you can see with the lists, you can start simple and build increasing complexity as you become more experienced.

Adding Toolbars with Sencha Touch

A common navigation metaphor for mobile devices is the toolbar. Either located at the top of the screen or at the bottom, the toolbar is a quick link tool that takes you to specific screens within your application, as shown in Figure 4.15.

As you might expect from your previous work with Sencha Touch, a toolbar is built from existing controls you are comfortable working with; specifically, the button control. The difference is that a toolbar groups a series of buttons together

Here is an example toolbar:

```
var buttonsGroup1 = [{
    text: 'Button One',
}, {
    text: 'Button Two',
}, {
    text: 'Round Three',
}
];
```

Figure 4.15 A set of several toolbars using Sencha Touch.

You can see that each button is a standard, square button. The difference is that the buttons are now in a group collecting them together as a toolbar.

In addition to the standard buttons you can you add specific, stylized buttons as defined by Sencha. Here you will see that the backward, forward, and rounded settings in the UI property have been set to change the visual appearance of the buttons in the toolbar:

```
var buttonsGroup1 = [{
    text: 'Back',
    ui: 'back',
}, {
    text: 'Default',
    badgeText: '2',
}, {
    text: 'Round',
    ui: 'round',
},
{
    text: 'Forward',
    ui: 'forward',
}];
```

Again, Sencha Touch is building complexity into fundamental functionality.

Enhancing Content on the Screen with the Carousel and Tabs

A challenge when developing solutions for devices such as the Android phone is how limited you are with the screen space. It doesn't matter if you have a Droid with a 4-inch screen or an iPhone 4—the screen space is just not that great. Sencha Touch provides you two tools you can use to control how users easily access large amounts of content: Carousel and Tabs.

The Carousel allows you to swipe from one screen to the next with each screen having its own set of data.

The Tabs control allows you to have tabs in your toolbar that show or hide different screens.

By now, you will recognize that the carousel is an xtype with items for the different screens. Following is a three-screen carousel. Each screen is defined by a cls to show it is a different screen, or card (the metaphor of breaking screens into cards comes from HP's webOS mobile operating system):

```
items: [{
    xtype: 'carousel',
    items: [{
        html: '<p>Navigate the carousel on this page by
swiping left/right.</p>',
```

```
                cls: 'card card1'
            },
            {
                html: '<p>Clicking on either side of the
    indicators below</p>',
                cls: 'card card2'
            },
            {
                html: 'Card #3',
                cls: 'card card3'
            }]
        }
```

This is just a basic example showing you how to insert a horizontal, side-swiping carousel. What is interesting, however, is that you can convert your carousel from horizontal to vertical by adding a single parameter called direction as shown:

```
    {
        xtype: 'carousel',
        ui: 'light',
        direction: 'vertical',
        items: [{
            html: '<p>A vertical carousel M</p> ',
            cls: 'card card1'
        },
        {
            html: 'Screen #2',
            cls: 'card card2'
        },
        {
            html: 'Screen #3',
            cls: 'card card3'
        }]
    }]
```

That's it. Your carousel has transformed from sliding horizontally to vertically, as shown in Figure 4.16.

Working with tabs is very similar to the carousel. You have actually already been introduced to the tab. We covered it in the first Sencha Touch app you created at the beginning of this article. In that example the page you created had only one tab. Let's expand that to three:

```
    demos.Tabs = new Ext.TabPanel({
        sortable: true, // Tap and hold to sort
        ui: 'dark',
        items: [{
            title: 'Tab 1',
            html: 'You can add your own HTML here with HTML5
    elements',
            cls: 'card card1'
        },
```

Figure 4.16 A carousel can have either vertical or horizontal scroll effects.

Figure 4.17 Using Sencha Touch to generate a tab navigation system.

```
    {
        title: 'Tab 2',
        html: 'Tab 2',
        cls: 'card card2'
    },
    {
        title: 'Tab 3',
        html: 'Tab 3',
        cls: 'card card3'
    }]
});
```

The first line defines the code as a TabPanel. The second line is a nifty property that allows you to drag and drop tabs. A user can select the tab on the iPhone and drag it to a new position.

Each tab is defined in the items section of the code. There are three critical elements for each tab definition: title, HTML, and cls. As you can see in Figure 4.17, this is similar to the carousel.

Controlling Video with Sencha Touch

Increasingly it is important to have video in your apps. As you might expect, Sencha Touch provides a tool that allows you to very easily add video. The Sencha Touch video player performs two functions: you can easily add video to the page and, second, leverage a prebuilt player that is consistent from one device to another.

As you might expect, the video control is an xtype with properties. Here is an example:

```
items: [{
    xtype: 'video',
    url: 'myVideo.mp4',
    loop: true,
posterUrl: 'myVideoPoster.png'
  }]
```

As you can see, the xtype is called 'video' in line two. A link to the video file is on the third line. The video itself can be set to loop. The final line points to an image that will act as a placeholder for the video before it starts playing.

When you are playing video you will want to make sure you use an MP4 video file format. At some point the Android OS will start to support WebM video, but iOS devices support only MPEG-4 formatted content.

Summary

In many ways, Sencha Touch is very different from competing mobile web frameworks. You build your web apps using JavaScript. The whole process is more "app-like" than jQuery Mobile or straight HTML5. And this is a good thing. It is becoming increasingly clear that web apps are a critical element of the future of mobile development. Sencha Touch fills that space between HTML and native app.

The next article will blur the difference between the web and native apps by allowing you to convert your web pages into native applications using a tool called PhoneGap.

PROJECT: BUILDING A WEB APPLICATION WITH SENCHA TOUCH

Sencha Touch is arguably the most complex web framework used in this book. There is a heavy reliance on JavaScript. The goal of this project is to present to you a tool that allows you to see a complete Sencha Touch project from A to Z.

In this project you will build a web application that identifies your location using geolocation in the mobile web browser, displays a Google Map of your location, and lists a stream of tweets in your area.

What You Will Need

To get started with this project you will need to download the files from *www.visualizetheweb.com*. The files for this project are contained in a ZIP file that you can extract on your desktop.

You will find a lot of project files. The two most important are index.html and index.js—these are the two files that drive your application.

Setting Up Your Sencha Touch Project: First, the HTML

The first document you will review is index.html. The file is constructed of the following:
- Reference to the Sencha Touch CSS
- Reference to custom CSS
- Google Map JavaScript file
- Sencha Touch JavaScript file
- Custom JavaScript

Here is the HTML from index.html:

```
<!DOCTYPE html>
<html>
<head>
  <meta http-equiv="Content-Type" content="text/html;
charset=utf-8">
  <title>Find Tweets</title>
  <!-- Sencha Touch CSS -->
  <link rel="stylesheet" href="css/sencha-touch.css"
type="text/css">
  <!-- Custom CSS -->
  <link rel="stylesheet" href="css/guide.css"
type="text/css">
  <!-- Google Maps JS -->
  <script type="text/javascript" src="http://maps.
google.com/maps/api/js?sensor=false"></script>
  <!-- Sencha Touch JS -->
  <script type="text/javascript" src="sencha-touch.
js"></script>
  <!-- Application JS -->
  <script type="text/javascript" src="src/index.js"></
script>
  <style>
    .refreshBtn {
      margin: 0 !important;
    }
  </style>
</head>
<body></body>
</html>
```

The HTML is merely a container to load the files needed in the project. This is common for all Sencha Touch projects. Figure P4.1 shows the application running on a mobile device.

Second: Custom CSS

The CSS has been extended for the project. What follows is a new collection of CSS that you can find in the file named guide.css. The file allows for the Twitter feeds to present correctly on the Tweet screen as shown in Figure P4.2.

```
.x-tabbar {
  padding-top: 10px !important;
  border-bottom: 2px solid #306aa1 !important;
}
.tweet {
  padding: 10px 0 10px 68px;
```

Figure P4.1 A Sencha Touch web app.

Figure P4.2 The customized user interface for the Twitter news stream.

```
  border-top: 1px solid #ccc;
  min-height: 68px;
  background-color: #fff;
}
.tweet h2 {
  font-weight: bold;
}
  .tweet .avatar {
     position: absolute;
     left: 10px;
}
.tweet .avatar img {
  max-width: 48px;
}
```

The next step is to review the JavaScript.

Third: The JavaScript

The first block of JavaScript sets up the project, the loading images, and the icon, and identifies the two different screens: Tweets and Your Location.

```
Ext.setup({
    tabletStartupScreen: 'tablet_startup.png',
    phoneStartupScreen: 'phone_startup.png',
    icon: 'icon.png',
    glossOnIcon: false,
    onReady: function() {
      var timeline = new Ext.Component({
    title: 'Tweets',
    cls: 'timeline',
    scroll: 'vertical',
    tpl: [
    '<tpl for=".">',
    '<div class="tweet">',
    '<div class="avatar"><img src="{profile_image_url}" />
</div>',
    '<div class="tweet-content">',
    '<h2>{from_user}</h2>',
    '<p>{text}</p>',
    '</div>',
    '</div>',
    '</tpl>'
    ]
    });
```

The following refreshes the screen and pulls your location from using the Geolocation class:

```
var refresh = function(position) {
var coords = position || map.geo.coords;
if (coords) {
  map.update(coords);
```

This takes your data and searches for information in your area from Twitter's news stream service:

```
Ext.util.JSONP.request({
   url: 'http://search.twitter.com/search.json',
   callbackKey: 'callback',
   params: {
geocode: coords.latitude + ',' + coords.longitude + ','
+ '5mi',
rpp: 30
   },
   callback: function(data) {
if (data && data.results && !!data.results.length) {
   data = data.results;
```

The following forces the Twitter timeline to update:

```
timeline.update(data);
```

The next section adds a point to the map to identify your location:

```
    for (var i = 0, ln = data.length; i < ln; i++) {
      addMarker(data[i]);
    }
  } else {
    timeline.getContentTarget().update('No Results
Available');
  } }});}};
```

The following section identifies your location as the default location for the Google Map screen:

```
    var map = new Ext.Map({
    title: 'Your Location',
    useCurrentLocation: true,
    mapOptions: {
    zoom: 11
    },
    listeners: {
    maprender: function(mapC, map) {
    refresh(this.geo.coords);
    this.geo.on('update', refresh);
    }
    }
      });
      ;
      var panel = new Ext.TabPanel({
    fullscreen: true,
    cardSwitchAnimation: 'slide',
    items: [map, timeline]
      });
```

The following leverages the Google Map APIs to add your position to the screen:

```
    var markers = {};
    var addMarker = function(tweet, position) {
    if (markers[tweet.from_user_id]) {
      return;
    }
    position = tweet.geo ? tweet.geo.coordinates: null;
    if (!position && tweet.location) {
      var L = String(tweet.location).split(':')[1] ||
tweet.location;
      position = L.split(',');
    }
    if (position) {
```

```
        markers[tweet.from_user_id] =
        new google.maps.Marker({
        map: map.map,
        title: tweet.from_user,
        position: new google.maps.LatLng(position[0],
position[1])
          });
      }
        };
```

The following adds the tabBar to the top of the screen:

```
        var tabBar = panel.gettabBar();
        tabBar.addDocked({
      cls: 'refreshBtn',
      xtype: 'button',
      ui: 'plain',
      iconMask: true,
      iconCls: 'refresh',
      dock: 'right',
      stretch: false,
      align: 'center',
      handler: refresh
        });
        panel.doComponentLayout();
        }
      });
```

Save your file.

At this time you have added all the custom code needed for your project. Move your files to your website and view the project through your favorite smart phone.

Summary

In this project you have seen how you can build a web app with Sencha Touch. The application allowed you to experiment with several key technologies such as:

- Geolocation
- Google Maps
- JSON data feeds
- Loading Twitter feeds
- Extending Sencha Touch CSS

There is a steep learning curve to Sencha Touch. The reward, however, is that you can build complex applications that leverage the latest APIs in your web browser, such as geolocation.

CONVERTING WEBSITES INTO NATIVE APPS USING PHONEGAP

Up to this point you have built sophisticated websites using HTML, CSS, and JavaScript. Mobile website development is only one of two distinct reasons customers have smart phones. The other reason is apps.

Apps are all the games, utilities, and programs you download onto your phone. Today there are over 300,000 different apps for Android and iOS. Other devices, such as BlackBerry, are building large libraries of applications. In other words, the app market is white hot, as shown in Figure 5.1.

So how do you get in?

This is the brilliant bit. You can use the CSS, HTML5, and JavaScript you have already been using. A company called Nitobi has developed a tool called PhoneGap that allows you to build apps using web technologies. There is no need to know complex programming languages such as Objective-C or Java.

In this section you will convert mobile websites into real-world applications for Android and iOS devices using PhoneGap.

Working with PhoneGap

To build an application for the iPhone, BlackBerry, or Android device requires you to work in a development environment that uses a specialized Software Developers Kit (SDK). For the iPhone, Apple has Xcode, a complete development environment; for Android, Google has an SDK that snaps into the open source Eclipse development environment.

Notobi's PhoneGap is a set of custom templates that work within these development environments. PhoneGap templates provide a set of default settings that do most of the work for you, as shown in Figure 5.2.

The advantage this gives you is that you are building directly in the development environment for the mobile operating system you are targeting, giving you access to all the testing and debugging tools that any developer will be using. In addition,

Figure 5.1 A wall of apps.

Figure 5.2 Notobi's PhoneGap deploys apps to all popular smart phone environments.

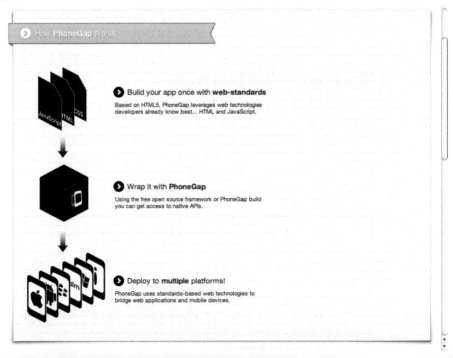

Nitobi has gone to great lengths to make it easy for you to work through the tools.

The negative is that you do need an understanding for how to build an application in the development environment. The term "build" is commonly used to describe the process of converting your code into a native application.

Each development platform has a different approach to building an application. PhoneGap's approach to building templates that install into the native development tools gives you a head start. Fundamentally, PhoneGap will be ready for you to use in your development tools in two steps:

1. Download and install the development environment.
2. Download and install PhoneGap templates.

Let's take Google's Android as an example. To run PhoneGap on Android, first you need to get to Google's developers website (developer.android.com). Select and download the development environment for Android for the operating system you are working on (you have a choice of Windows, Mac, or Linux).

Go to *http://eclipse.org/* and select the Download Eclipse button. The file will download. After the files have downloaded, run the installation to install Eclipse. After Eclipse has installed, you can add the PhoneGap files.

Go to PhoneGap.com and select the Download button. You will be downloading a ZIP file containing the PhoneGap templates, as shown in Figure 5.3.

Figure 5.3 PhoneGap can be downloaded in one file.

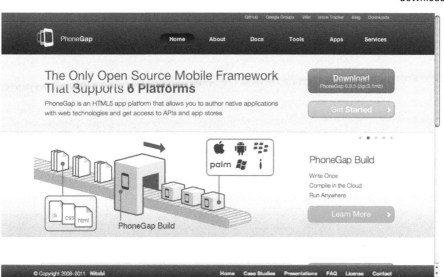

Expanding the ZIP file will reveal a set of subfolders:

- WebOS
- BlackBerry
- Android
- Bada
- iOS
- Symbian

Each folder is tied directly to a mobile operating system. An additional folder named Documentation provides detailed explanation for all the supported features within PhoneGap, as shown in Figure 5.4.

Open the Android folder. You will see a folder named Sample. The Sample folder is a blank project that you can open and use as a template for future projects. Within Sample, look for the subfolder named Assets and then www.

The www folder is where you can place your HTML, CSS, and JavaScript. You can install any HTML5 that is supported by the browser on the Android Phone. This includes advanced technologies such as geolocation, web storage, and CSS3.

Once you have copied over your files, you can use the build tools that are built into Android. In this chapter we will not delve too deeply into the Android build process. You can find a lot of information converting the details of application build for Android at Google's Android YouTube Channel, at *www.youtube.com/user/androiddevelopers* (Figure 5.5).

Arguably one of the most complex environments is Apple's iOS development process; it is also the platform where you will

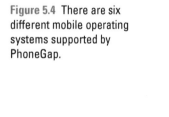

Figure 5.4 There are six different mobile operating systems supported by PhoneGap.

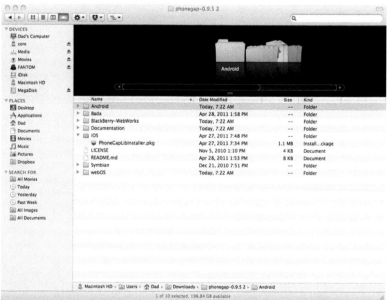

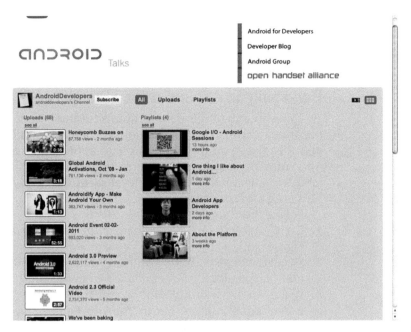

Figure 5.5 Google's Android Developer Channel on YouTube.

get a significant number of downloads. For this reason, we are going to step through in detail the process of building an application using Apple's Xcode.

Setting Up a PhoneGap Project for iOS Devices

Apple's development process is complex. There are benefits and negatives to this. On one hand you have process that is thorough and can accurately trace back all applications to the original developer. The negative is that building an application for the iPhone can be a time-consuming process.

The development environment for iOS is Xcode. Before you even download and install Xcode you will need to complete the following steps to become a certified developer and have your apps registered with Apple.

Becoming an Apple Developer

To create an iPhone app you need to complete several activities before your apps will run:
1. Become a certified Apple developer.
2. Create a development and a Developer P12 certificate.
3. Register your development iPhone with Apple.

The hardest part of developing apps for the iPhone is not the code you will develop, but ensuring you have all of your is and ts dotted and crossed per Apple's rigorous registration process.

Becoming an Apple Certified Developer

To be able to develop applications for the iPhone you need to become a certified Apple developer. The cost is only $99 a year and this gives you the ability to load applications to the iTunes App Store. Yes, you heard me correctly—it costs only $99 a year to load as many apps as you can develop into the iTunes App Store. This is an amazing deal.

Follow these steps:

1. On a Mac go to *http://developer.apple.com/ios* as shown in Figure 5.6.
2. Select the Register button. Either use the iTunes Account information you already have or create a new account.
3. When you have completed the registration you will be sent an e-mail containing a link to your developer and distribution certificates.
4. Go to *https://developer.apple.com/devcenter/ios/index.action* to download and install an Apple iPhone Developer Certificate.
5. View the certificate by opening Keychain on your Mac. You will need to reference the two certificates as you develop your iPhone Apps.
6. Right-click the Developer Certificate. Select Export Certificate.

Figure 5.6 Apple's iOS Dev Center.

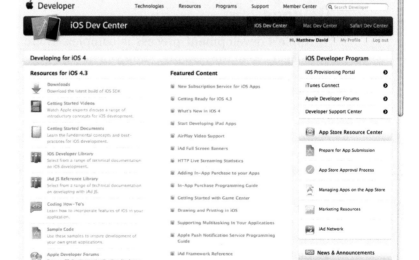

7. Select a place where you want to save the certificate. Use the P12 Personal Information Exchange format.
8. Select the Save button. You will be prompted to give your app a password. Give it a secure password and remember it—you will need it later.
9. Export the Distribution certificate in P12 format, too.

After you have your P12 certificates you will need to register your test iPhone with Apple. You can register up to 100 devices per year.

1. Connect your test iPhone/iPod Touch to your computer.
2. Open iTunes and select your device from the list to view the Summary tab data.
3. Click the serial number next to your device. The number will change to an identifier (UDID) number.
4. Copy the number.
5. Go to *http://developer.apple.com/ios/manage/devices/index. action* as shown in Figure 5.7.
6. Select Add Devices.
7. On the Add Devices screen paste in the UDID number and give your device a name. You may want to choose something like "iPhone Development" or "iPod Touch Gen 3 Development."

The developer account ID, registered device, and P12 certificates are needed for all apps your want to sell in the iTunes App Store.

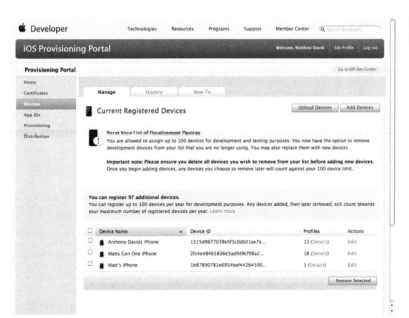

Figure 5.7 iOS Device management.

Preparing to Develop an App

Each iPhone app you develop requires several specific tools for it to work. They include:

- App ID
- Provisioning profile
- Icons

With these three tasks complete you will able to create iPhone apps.

Creating App IDs

The App ID is a unique identifier Apple uses to identify your app from the tens of thousands of apps in the iTunes App Store.

1. Go to the App ID page in the iOS developer center (*http://developer.apple.com/ios/manage/bundles/index.action*) as shown in Figure 5.8.
2. Select New App ID.
3. Give your new app ID a name you can find easily, such as ShakespeareQuotes. The name has to be all one word.
4. Finally, you need to add a bundle seed ID. The convention is to reverse your website address and add the app's name at the end. For instance, com.focalpress.ShakespeareQuotes.
5. Select OK and your new App ID is ready for you.

With your App ID created you can create a provisioning profile for your app.

Figure 5.8 App ID management.

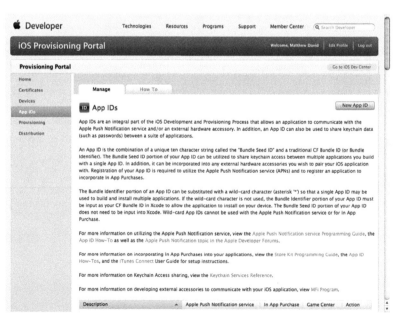

Creating a Developer's Provisioning Profile

A provisioning profile is a document that you associate with your app for either development or for iTunes app distribution. There are three types of provisioning profiles: Developer, Distribution to Ad Hoc, and Distribution to iTunes App Store. We will cover how to use the Distribution Profiles later in the chapter. For now, you will focus on creating the Developer Profile.

1. Go to the Profile page in the iPhone developer center (*http:// developer.apple.com/ios/manage/provisioningprofiles/index. action*) as shown in Figure 5.9.
2. Select the Development tag.
3. Select New profile.
4. Give your profile a meaningful name. A convention that is gaining popularity is to use the prefix "dev" followed by the App ID; for instance, DevMyFirstApp.
5. From the Certificates list check your name.
6. Find your App ID from the drop-down list.
7. Select your test device from the devices listed and then select the Submit button.
8. Your certificate will take about 30 seconds to generate. When it has, you will see a Download button. Select the Download button and save the Developer Profile to your desktop. The file should have the extension mobileprovision.
9. Connect your test iPhone to iTunes.
10. Drag the downloaded Developer Profile onto iTunes and then sync your iPhone. This adds the Developer Profile to your testing device.

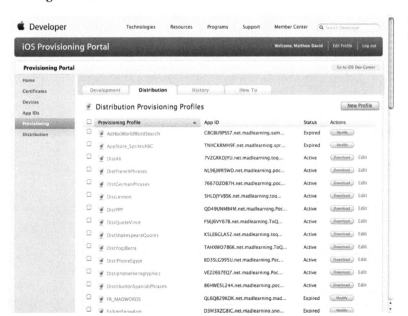

Figure 5.9 Apple's provisioning site.

Developing Icons for Your iPhone Apps

In preparation for your iPhone app you need four PNG images:
- 29.png—a file that is 29 × 29 pixels
- 57.png—a file that is 57 × 57 pixels
- 512.png—a file that is 512 × 512 pixels
- Default.png—a placeholder file that is used while your app is loading. The file must start with a capital D.

You can create all of these files using tools such as Adobe Fireworks.

Building Your App with Xcode

Now you have all documents you need for an application, but you also need the development environment. Apple's development environment is Xcode.

As a licensed member of the Apple iOS Developer program you can download Xcode for free from developer.apple.com/ios. Xcode is a very large file, so it will take a while to download.

Installing Xcode is the same as any software package on OS X. Before you start Xcode, you need to install the PhoneGap Xcode templates. From the PhoneGap.zip you downloaded earlier, locate the subfolder named iOS. Open the folder and locate the file named PhoneGapLibInstaller.pkg, as shown in Figure 5.10.

Double-click on PhoneGapLibInstaller.pkg to install the template file. Locate the profile you created for your app site and drag the profile onto the Xcode icon. This adds the profile to Xcode and will allow you to associate it with your app later.

When the PhoneGap files have been installed, open Xcode. On the Xcode splash screen, select the New Project button to choose a new project.

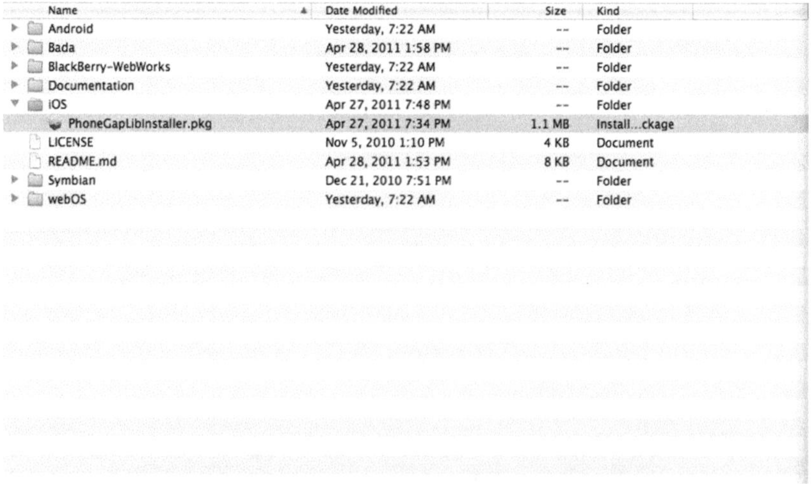

Figure 5.10 The iOS version of PhoneGap.

Name	Date Modified	Size	Kind
▶ Android	Yesterday, 7:22 AM	--	Folder
▶ Bada	Apr 28, 2011 1:58 PM	--	Folder
▶ BlackBerry-WebWorks	Yesterday, 7:22 AM	--	Folder
▶ Documentation	Yesterday, 7:22 AM	--	Folder
▼ iOS	Apr 27, 2011 7:48 PM	--	Folder
PhoneGapLibInstaller.pkg	Apr 27, 2011 7:34 PM	1.1 MB	Install...ckage
LICENSE	Nov 5, 2010 1:10 PM	4 KB	Document
README.md	Apr 28, 2011 1:53 PM	8 KB	Document
▶ Symbian	Dec 21, 2010 7:51 PM	--	Folder
▶ webOS	Yesterday, 7:22 AM	--	Folder

The New Project screen opens. Along the left-hand side you will see PhoneGap under the User Templates category, as shown in Figure 5.11.

Choose the default PhoneGap-based application.

Xcode now generates the files needed for the project. This only takes a moment. To make your project tied to your app, you will need to make a couple of settings changes.

From the Project menu select Edit Project Settings. The settings screen has four main sections: General, Build, Configurations, and Comments, as shown in Figure 5.12.

Select the Build section. You need to associate the profile for your app with this project. This is done in the section named Code Signing with the property Code Signing Identity.

To the right of the Code Signing Identity property is a drop-down menu you can select that allows you to choose from the profiles you have associated with Xcode. Select the appropriate profile.

At this time you can close the Settings screen. Associating the profiles is a process you only have to complete once per year.

The next configuration step is to modify the Plist configuration document for your project. The application Plist is located in the main project under the Resources subfolder. You will see two Plist files, one named PhoneGap.plist and the second named after your app. Do not modify the PhoneGap.plist document. Select the Plist for your app. You will see that the Plist is a set of properties with values, as shown in Figure 5.13.

Figure 5.11 Choosing PhoneGap in Xcode.

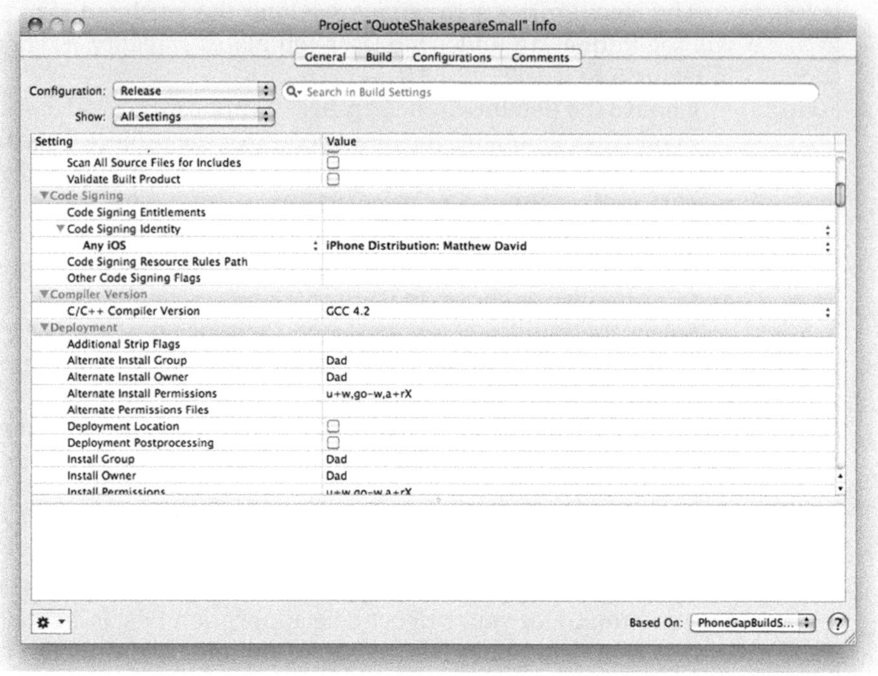

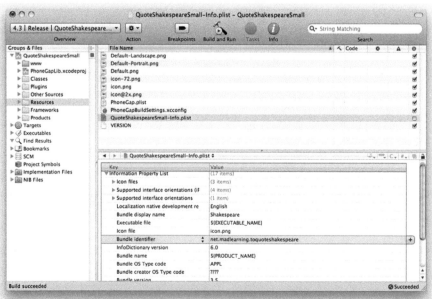

Figure 5.12 Xcode project
settings.

Figure 5.13 Your apps Plist
settings.

Locate the property named Bundle identifier; the bundle identifier is the full conical name of your app. You already set this when you created your app ID on Apple's developer website. You will need to write the full name here. For instance, using the example App ID from before would be com.focalpress.ShakespeareQuotes.

At this point, you have completed all the default settings for your app. Here is the good news: you do not need to go through these steps again. How about that?

Now onto the fun stuff: creating apps with HTML.

In your Xcode project you will see a subfolder named www. By default the folder contains the the the file Index.html.

At this time you can build your app. Go to the Build menu option and choose Build and Run. The default setting in Xcode is to install your app in the iPhone Simulator that comes with Xcode. You now have an app. OK, it doesn't show anything, but it is a real app. Close the Simulator to kill the test. Go back to Xcode and select the folder named www. Right-click on the folder and choose Reveal in Finder. The OS X Finder opens showing you the folder for the HTML files.

Now you can add your own website files including images, video, HTML5, JavaScript, and CSS. There is no need to learn any Objective-C to build your application.

After you have added your files you can go back and test your app in Xcode in the Simulator. Voilà! One real-world iOS app built with HTML.

Extending PhoneGap with Plug-ins

The PhoneGap architecture has matured to the point where it now supports plug-ins. Essentially, a plug-in is a specialized piece of code that you can add to your project. Once it has been added you can connect to the plug-in with some JavaScript in your page.

Using plug-ins for PhoneGap can be a great way to extend the functionality of your app. But there are some caveats when working with plug-ins:

- Plug-ins are not created the same way for each Mobile OS platform. Each is custom-code tailored to the target device.
- All of the plug-ins are created as Open Source solutions.
- Each PhoneGap plug-in has different degrees of support.

Bottom line: plug-ins can be great but you will need to work through the idiosyncrasies of each plug-in yourself.

The best location to find plug-ins is GitHub at *https://github.com/phonegap/phonegap-plugins/* (see Figure 5.14).

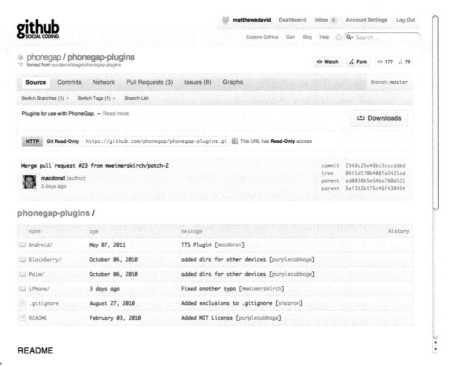

Figure 5.14 Plug-ins for PhoneGap.

There are currently four main categories of plug-ins:

- Android
- BlackBerry
- Palm (WebOS)
- iPhone

Each category has plug-ins customized to the operating system. Adding the plug-ins to your projects is similar. Within each PhoneGap project folder is a subfolder named Plugins. Here you will add the plug-ins for most of your projects. In your index.html file you will add JavaScript that allows you to link to Plugin.

The following is an example of using the MapKit plug-in for iOS development, as shown in Figure 5.15: *https://github.com/ phonegap/phonegap-plugins/blob/master/iPhone/MapKitPlug.*

To add the plug-in, you will need to download the following Objective-C files (*https://github.com/phonegap/phonegap-plugins/ tree/master/iPhone*):

- AsyncImageView.h
- AsyncImageView.m
- MapKit.h
- MapKit.m
- PGAnnotation.h
- PGAnnotation.m

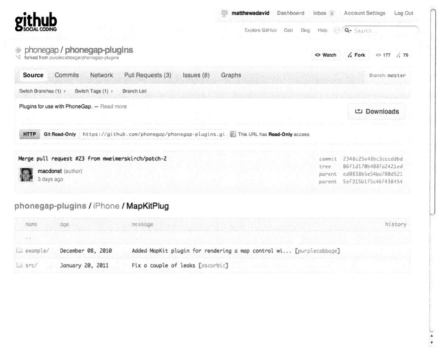

Figure 5.15 The MapKit plug-in.

These files should be added to the Plugins folder in your Xcode.

An additional JavaScript file called MapKitPlug.js needs to be added to the www folder that links the Objective-C to the HTML files.

At this point you have all the files you need to add a map to your web page. The map is tied directly back to Apple's native MapKit built into the iPhone.

The following HTML will add a MapKit map to your page:

```
<!DOCTYPE HTML PUBLIC "-//W3C//DTD HTML 4.01//EN"
"http://www.w3.org/TR/html4/strict.dtd">
  <html>
    <head>
```

Change this if you want to allow scaling:

```
<meta name="viewport" content="width=default-width;
user-scalable=no" />
    <meta http-equiv="Content-type" content="text/html;
charset=utf-8">
    <title>MapTest</title>
  iPad/iPhone specific css below, add after your main:
    <link rel="stylesheet" media="only screen and (max-
device-width: 1024px)" href="ipad.css" type="text/css" />
    <link rel="stylesheet" media="only screen and (max-
device-width: 480px)" href="iphone.css" type="text/css" />
```

The following adds links to both the PhoneGap and MapKit-Plugin JavaScript files:

```
<script type="text/javascript" charset="utf-8"
src="phonegap.js"></script>
<script type="text/javascript" charset="utf-8"
src="MapKitPlug.js"></script>
<script type="text/javascript" charset="utf-8">
function onBodyLoad()
{
document.addEventListener("deviceready",onDeviceReady,
false);
}
function cbMapCallback()
{
    alert(arguments[0]);
}
```

When this function is called, PhoneGap has been initialized and is ready to roll:

```
function onDeviceReady()
{
}
function showMap()
{
    var pin = { lat:49.281468,
                lon:-123.104446,
                title:"Nitobi HQ",
                pinColor:"purple",
                index:0,
                selected:true};
```

This runs the calls to MapKit:

```
var _options = {
    buttonCallback: "cbMapCallback",
    height:360,
    diameter:1000,
    atBottom:true,
    lat:pin.lat,
    lon:pin.lon
        };
window.plugins.mapKit.showMap();
window.plugins.mapKit.setMapData([pin],_options);
}
function hideMap()
{
    window.plugins.mapKit.hideMap();
}
function resizeMap()
{
```

```
var pin = { lat:49.281468,
            lon:-123.104446,
            title:"Nitobi HQ",
            pinColor:"purple",
            index:0,
            selected:true};
// do your thing!
var _options = {
    buttonCallback: "cbMapCallback",
     height:260,
     diameter:1000,
     atBottom:true,
     lat:pin.lat,
     lon:pin.lon
        };
window.plugins.mapKit.showMap();
window.plugins.mapKit.setMapData([pin],_options);
}
</script>
</head>
```

The following command in the BODY element loads MapKit into your HTML:

```
<body onload="onBodyLoad()">
    <button style="top:400px;position:absolute;"
onclick="showMap()">Show Map</button>
    <button style="left:100px;top:400px;position:
absolute;" onclick="hideMap()">Hide Map</button>
    <button style="left:200px;top:400px;position:
absolute;" onclick="resizeMap()">Resize Map</button>
  </body>
</html>
```

You can save and test your file. Without having to learn Objective-C and leveraging the JavaScript knowledge you already have you can load a native MapKit map into your app.

Extending PhoneGap with Custom Code

There will be times when you want to enhance the PhoneGap project you are working on using your own custom code. This can be done with PhoneGap—after all, you are building the solution in a native development environment. You have full access to the native code in that environment.

The following example will add Apple's iAd advertising feature to your app.

The first step is to add the iAd framework to your project. In your project folder you will see a category named Frameworks. Right-click on the folder and select Add → Add Existing Framework. From the pop-up window choose the framework named iAd.

Now you have to modify two Class files in your project. Go to your project and select the folder named Classes.

You will see two Class files that are labeled after your project name with the extension of either AppDelegate.h or AppDelegate.m. Select AppDelegate.h and modify the code to the following:

```
#import <UIKit/UIKit.h>
#import "PhoneGapDelegate.h"
#import <iAd/iAD.h>
@interface appNameDelegate : PhoneGapDelegate
<ADBannerViewDelegate> {
        BOOL bannerIsVisible;
    }
    @end
```

The important element is the inclusion of line three where you are importing the iAd framework.

The fourth and fifth line will bind the Objective-C code you will need to add to the delegate file. The file that ends in .m is where you will add your Objective-C to control the appearance of the iAd feature:

```
- (id) init
{
return [super init];
}
```

This is the main kick-off after the app inits; the views and settings are set up here.

```
- (void)applicationDidFinishLaunching:(UIApplication *)
application
    {
        [ super applicationDidFinishLaunching:application ];
    }
-(id) getCommandInstance:(NSString*)className
    {
```

You can catch your own commands here, if you wanted to extend the app protocol, or add your own app specific protocol to it.

```
return [super getCommandInstance:className];
    }
```

Called when the webview finishes loading, this stops the activity view and closes the image view:

```
- (void)webViewDidFinishLoad:(UIWebView *)theWebView
    {
        bannerIsVisible = YES;
        ADBannerView *adView = [[ADBannerView alloc]
initWithFrame:CGRectZero];
        adView.frame = CGRectMake(0, 430, 320, 50);
```

If you want the banner to be on top of the screen, remove these lines:

```
    adView.delegate = self;
    adView.currentContentSizeIdentifier = ADBannerContent
SizeIdentifier320x50;
       [theWebView addSubview:adView];
       return [ super webViewDidFinishLoad:theWebView ];}

  - (void)webViewDidStartLoad:(UIWebView *)theWebView
  {
     return [ super webViewDidStartLoad:theWebView ];
  }
  - (void)webView:(UIWebView *)theWebView
didFailLoadWithError:(NSError *)error
  {
    return [ super webView:theWebView
didFailLoadWithError:error ];
  }
  - (BOOL)webView:(UIWebView *)theWebView shouldStartLoadWit
hRequest:(NSURLRequest *)request navigationType:(UIWebViewNav
igationType)navigationType
  {
    return [ super webView:theWebView shouldStartLoadWithReq
uest:request navigationType:navigationType ];
  }
  - (BOOL) execute:(InvokedUrlCommand*)command
  {
    return [ super execute:command];
  }
```

This is where the AdBanner is called:

```
  - (void)bannerView:(ADBannerView *)banner didFailToReceive
AdWithError:(NSError *)error
  {
     if (bannerIsVisible)
  {
          [UIView beginAnimations:@"animateAdBannerOff"
context:NULL];
```

The preceding code assumes the banner view is at the bottom of the screen.

```
        banner.frame = CGRectOffset(banner.frame, 0, 50);
  [UIView commitAnimations];
        bannerIsVisible = NO;
     }
  }
  - (void)bannerViewDidLoadAd:(ADBannerView *)banner
  {
     if (!bannerIsVisible)
     {
        [UIView beginAnimations:@"animateAdBannerOn"
context:NULL];
```

This assumes the banner view is offset –50 pixels so that it is not visible.

```
        banner.frame = CGRectOffset(banner.frame, 0, -50);
[UIView commitAnimations];
        bannerIsVisible = YES;
    }
}
- (BOOL)bannerViewActionShouldBegin:(ADBannerView *)banner
willLeaveApplication:(BOOL)willLeave
    {
        NSLog(@"Banner view is beginning an ad action");
        BOOL shouldExecuteAction = YES;
```

Your app implements this method if you want it not fixed:

```
        if (!willLeave && shouldExecuteAction)
        {
```

Here you can insert code to suspend any services that might conflict with the advertisement.

```
    }
    return shouldExecuteAction;
}
- (void)dealloc
{
    [ super dealloc ];
}
@end
```

At this point you can save your files and test your app in the iPhone simulator. You will see that a sample ad runs. You cannot get real ads until you publish your app to the iTunes App Store.

Now you have an opportunity to monetize your applications.

Packaging Your App for the iTunes App Store

Apple's iTunes Store is an amazing success story: 300,000 apps and 7 billion downloads is nothing to sneeze at. There are many success stories of groups making millions from Apple. But, before you can get any money, you need to have your app ready for deployment.

At this time your app is ready for deployment to the iTunes App Store. There are some simple changes to your Xcode environment you need to make in order to publish your application.

With Xcode open to the project you are working on, you should make the following changes:

• The build must be targeted to a device.
• The Active Configuration in the build must be Release.

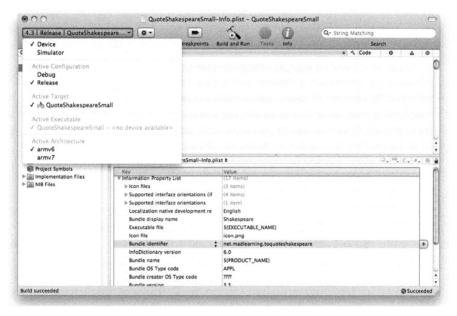

Figure 5.16 Packaging your app for distribution.

When you have these two settings applied, you can then go to Build → Build And Archive. This step will create a special version of your app that can be submitted directly to iTunes App Store, as shown in Figure 5.16.

Now your website is converted into an app and ready for submission. You will see that it is now being managed in the Organizer, as shown in Figure 5.17.

Figure 5.17 The Xcode App Organizer.

The final step is to go into Apple's iTunes Connect to configure the settings that will allow your app to appear in the App Store.

Using iTunes Connect to Publish Your App

You are now very close to having an app available on the iTunes store. Can you feel the rush? You could be selling thousands of apps in a matter of a few days. The gap between you and riches is Apple's iTunes Connect publishing tool. You will be using a new website to upload your final iPhone Apps. The site is called iTunes Connect (*https://itunesconnect.apple.com/*), as shown in Figure 5.18.

In every sense, iTunes Connect is your business relationship with Apple. The site allows you to set up your contracts, tax records, and banking information; review sales trends; download financial reports; and manage your In App Purchases. In App Purchases is a method for buying something within an app for iOS devices. You will need to complete these sections in order to sell your app in iTunes. This section is going to focus on the important part of iTunes Connect: managing your applications.

Figure 5.18 Apple's iTunes Connect is your business relationship with Apple.

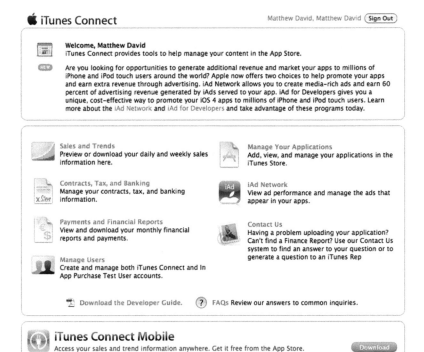

There are some tasks you can complete before you upload your app:

1. You will need at least one screen shot of your app as it appears in your iPhone. Fortunately there is a very easy way to do that. At any time when your app is playing on your iPhone, press the Home and Sleep buttons at the same time. The screen will flash and a screen shot will be taken of your app. The image is stored in your Camera Roll and is exactly the same size Apple needs.

2. When you have completed this task, go to *https://itunesconnect. apple.com*. Use your Apple Developer ID and Password to log into the site.

3. Select Manage Your App from iTunes Connect. You will be taken to a screen where you can add a new app and review apps you are selling.

4. Select the Add New App button to start the process of creating a new iTunes App.

5. There are several screens you need to complete to upload your app to iTunes. The first is the Export Compliance screen asking if the app contains encrypted data. You will want to keep your first app deployed to the App Store simple and not use encryption. Later, when you are familiar with the idiosyncrasies of the App Store submission process, you can experiment with different settings. Your first app should not have any encryption, so choose No at this time.

6. The next page is the Overview page. For the most part, the content you enter on this screen can be edited after your app has been submitted. There are two sections that cannot change: Application Name and Keywords. Ensure that you select a name that accurately describes what you selling. You are allowed up 100 characters of keywords. Use your Search Engine Optimization experience to add keywords that categorize your app. These two sections are very important.

7. The remaining fields allow you to add a description; submit the app to main categories; add copyright, version number (start with 1.0), SKU number, and application/support URL; and support e-mail. Select the Continue button when you have completed the page.

8. The next page allows you to add a Rating for your app. A rating is determined by answering 10 questions. Click the Continue button when you have answered the questions to take you to the Upload page.

9. Upload the 512.jpg for the large icon.

10. Upload a 480 × 320 jpg image for the primary screenshot.

11. Add one to four 480 × 320 jpg images for the additional screenshots. You will get a green check mark for each successfully loaded image.

12. Select Continue to go to the Pricing and Availability screen.
13. You do not get to select a specific price for your app. Instead, Apple lists a number of Tiers you can choose. At first glance this may seem frustrating but what Apple has done is to remove the pain of selling with different currencies. A Tier 2 app will be $0.99 in the United States, 59 pence in England, and AU$1.29 in Australia. There are over 70 different currencies that Apple manages for you. You can also choose to have screens that show the app going on sale in different countries.
14. The availability option allows your app to go on sale at a specific time in the future.
15. At this point you get to review all of your content and press the Submit button.
16. When the meta-content has been saved you can go back to your Xcode Organizer and find the app you have been working on. Select the latest build version and choose the Submit button.
17. A window will open asking you to match your app with a profile on iTunes Connect. Select the correct profile and submit your app.

Apple has done a lot to improve the review process for new apps. Today it only takes five to seven days for an app to be approved by Apple and appear in iTunes.

Using Dreamweaver CS5.5 to Build Your PhoneGap Projects

Adobe has gone full onboard for its support of both HTML5 and Mobile development. To this end, starting with the release of Dreamweaver CS5.5 you can now natively support iOS and Android PhoneGap.

Creating a PhoneGap app in Dreamweaver is as simple as extending site settings. Adobe has a number of videos on its website (*http://tv.adobe.com/*) that step you through the process of converting Dreamweaver from a web development tool into an app machine.

Using PhoneGap Build to Create BlackBerry and Windows Phone Apps

A third place you can build your PhoneGap app is with the newly released PhoneGap Build. Located at build.phonegap.com the new service allows you to upload your files directly to the Cloud and have PhoneGap's build servers convert your HTML into native apps, as shown in Figure 5.19.

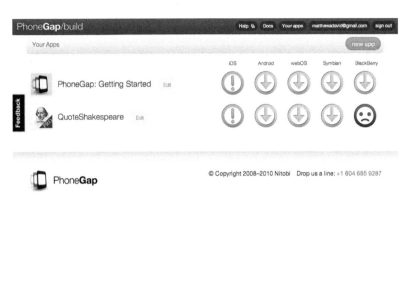

Figure 5.19 PhoneGap Build.

Using Build allows you to target multiple OS environments without having to have a deep knowledge of each OS SDK and tools.

Summary

The world has gone app crazy. There is a very good reason: Apps make money. In this section you have seen how you can take your knowledge of HTML5 for mobile devices and convert your optimized websites into native applications that run on Android, iPhones, BlackBerrys, and more.

PhoneGap integrates tightly into the development environment you are working in. The benefit this bring is that you can extend the core codebase in your apps with plug-ins and extensions. This gives you the opportunity to leverage features such as such as maps, advertising, and more.

The popularity of PhoneGap has reached the ears of many companies. In particular, Adobe is now including PhoneGap support starting with Dreamweaver CS5.5. If you do not have Dreamweaver you can use a web service called PhoneGap Build that will convert your HTML files into native apps. There simply is no excuse when it comes to creating apps: If you know HTML, then you can build a native application.

PROJECT: BUILDING A NATIVE iOS APP WITH PHONEGAP

Throughout the book we have been talking about building web-sites for mobile devices. This is great, but there is one next step you need to take: building native applications.

PhoneGap is emerging as a leading tool for converting applications from HTML into native applications. In this project you will convert a mobile website into a native application for Android, iOS, and BlackBerry phones.

What You Will Need

To get started with this project you will need to download the files from *www.visualizetheweb.com*. The files for this project are contained in a ZIP file that you can extract on your desktop.

The project files you need to build this project include the following:
• Icons
• Web app with iUI framework

Setting Up Your Web Files for the Project

The first step in converting a website into a PhoneGap native application is to create your web content. For this example you will use a mobile website that is a collection of quotes from Buddha, as shown in Figure P5.1.

While stepping through the code for the Buddha web app you will see that a new code base is being used: iUI. iUI is an lesser known alternative to jQuery Mobile. The framework can be down-loaded at *http://code.google.com/p/iui/downloads/list*.

The framework is a great alternative to jQTouch. You can download the files at *http://www.iui-js.org/*.

Figure P5.1 iUI is used as the mobile framework.

Figure P5.2 The iUI website.

You will want to edit the folder labeled www. Expand the folder to see the files contained within. The key elements are:

- PhoneGap.js
- CSS folder (containing the theme)
- iUI folder (containing iUI assets)
- SpryAssets (dataset files)
- index.html
- quote.html

Let's look at the index.html page. The HTML in the HEADER element consists of the following:

```
<html>
<head>
<title>To Quote Buddha</title>
```

The opening HTML declares that the document is using HTML5. The TITLE element will be ignored when you publish these pages as a native app (I added it through habit).

The following line declares the size of the page as it relates to a viewport. The viewport is a specific Meta attribute Apple introduced with iOS.

```
<meta name="viewport" content="width=device-width;
initial-scale=1.0; maximum-scale=1.0; user-scalable=0;"/>
```

The following META element is another specific Apple iOS attribute that allows the web page to run as a web app.

```
<meta name="apple-mobile-web-app-capable" content="yes"
/>
```

The following SCRIPT element links to an Adobe JavaScript framework called Spry. The Spry framework allows the application to load external data into the web pages. This is very useful for managing your content.

```
<script src="SpryAssets/SpryData.js" type="text/
javascript"></script>
<script src="SpryAssets/SpryHTMLDataSet.js" type="text/
javascript"></script>
<link href="SpryAssets/SpryMasterDetail.css"
rel="stylesheet" type="text/css" />
<script type="text/javascript">
var ds1 = new Spry.Data.HTMLDataSet("quote.html",
"quotes", {sortOnLoad: "LeadIn", sortOrderOnLoad:
"ascending"});
ds1.setColumnType("Quote", "html");
</script>
```

The following points to the iUI CSS and JavaScript frameworks:

```
<link rel="stylesheet" href="iui/iui.css" type="text/
css" />
<link rel="stylesheet" title="Default" href="iui/t/
default/default-theme.css" type="text/css"/>
<link rel="stylesheet" href="css/iui-panel-list.css"
type="text/css" />
<script type="application/x-javascript" src="iui/iui.
js"></script>
</head>
<body>
```

These frameworks point to the libraries, CSS, and data sources you will use in your application. The following sets the web pages themselves. As with jQTouch and jQuery Mobile, you will see that the DIV element is used to manage how content is presented on the screen. The following is the toolbar across the top of the screen:

```
<div class="toolbar">
  <h1 id="pageTitle"></h1>
  <a id="backButton" class="button" href="#"></a> </div>
<ul id="home" title="To Quote..." selected="true">
```

```
<li><a href="#quotes">Buddha's Quotes</a></li>
<li><a href="#bio">Buddha's Bio</a></li>
<li><a href="#about">About</a></li>
</ul><br /><br /><br />
</div>
```

You will see that a standard HTML list is used to separate content with links to the different screens. The same metaphor is used with other mobile frameworks.

The following DIV elements manage the dynamic data pulled into the application. For this project we will not go into too much detailed regarding how this is managed with the Spry framework.

```
<div id="quotes" class="panel">
 <h2>Buddha's Quotes</h2>
 <span spry:region="ds1" class="listClass">
   <ul id="quotes" selected="true" >
     <li spry:repeat="ds1" spry:setrow="ds1" ><a
href="#quote">{LeadIn}</a></li>
   </ul><br /><br /><br />
 </span>
</div>
```

Each quote can be viewed in its own screen. The following is the HTML to create this screen:

```
<div id="quote" class="panel">
 <div spry:detailregion="ds1" class="DetailContainer">
<h2>{LeadIn}</h2>
 <p class="DetailColumn">{Quote}</p>
 <br>
 <p class="DetailColumn">Author: {Author}</p><br /><br />
<br />
 </div>
</div>
```

The next two screens are the standard "about the app" screens you find in many applications:

```
<div id="bio" class="panel">
 <h2>The History Of Buddha</h2>
 <p class="DetailColumn">
 <p>Siddhartha Gautama was a spiritual teacher from
ancient India who founded Buddhism. In most Buddhist
traditions, he is regarded as the Supreme Buddha
(P. sammambuddha, S. samyaksabuddha) of our age, "Buddha"
meaning "awakened one" or "the enlightened one." The time
of his birth and death are uncertain: most early 20th-
century historians dated his lifetime as c. 563 BCE to 483
BCE, but more recent opinion may be dating his death to
between 411 and 400 BCE.
 </P>
```

```
    <p>Gautama, also known as Sakyamuni ("Sage of the
Sakyas"), is the primary figure in Buddhism, and accounts
of his life, discourses, and monastic rules are believed
by Buddhists to have been summarized after his death
and memorized by his followers. Various collections of
teachings attributed to him were passed down by oral
tradition, and first committed to writing about 400 years
later.
        </p>
    <p class="DetailColumn">Source: Wikipedia.org</p><br />
<br /><br />
    </div>
    <div id="about" class="panel">
      <h2>About</h2>
    <p class="DetailColumn">"To Quote Buddha" is a MAD
Learning education app designed for parents by parents</p>
    <p align="center"><a href="mailto:info@madlearning.
net">info@madlearning.net</a></p>
    <p align="center"><a href="http://www.madlearning.net"
target="_blank">www.madlearning.net</a></p>
    </body>
    </html>
```

At this point you have the entire HTML you need to run this page. You can test the HTML by loading the page into Safari or a similar web browser.

Using PhoneGap Build

Creating the HTML is the first part of converting your files into a native app. The next step is to use your code to create the native application. This can be done a number of ways. Arguably the easiest way is to use a service such as PhoneGap's Build service, as shown in Figure P5.3.

You can access the Build service at *https://build.phonegap.com/*.

At this time, PhoneGap's Build service allows you to create native applications for the following:

- iOS (iPhone/iPad)
- Android
- WebOS
- BlackBerry
- Symbian
- Windows Phone 7
- MeeGo
- Bada

The last three mobile operating systems were not available at the time of writing this book, but a sneak peak lets me know that they will be supported by the time you read this book.

Figure P5.3 PhoneGap Build.

You will need to register with PhoneGap's Build site to create an account. Following the creation of a new account you will also need to create digital certificates for iOS, BlackBerry, and Android applications. This is one-time-only process. There is a lot of help information on PhoneGap's site for this process. Give yourself a full day to make sure you complete the certificate process correctly. Again, once you have done this you will not need to do it again. Phew!

Building Your Application

Nitobi has made the process for building your applications very easy. There are three ways to convert a collection of web pages into an app:

- Create a new GIT repository
- Pull from an existing git/svn project (you will need to provide the exact URL)
- Package a collection of web pages into a ZIP file and upload to the cloud service

I prefer to use the third method. All you have to do is select the main folder for your files and convert it into a ZIP file. For Mac users this means right-clicking and selecting the Archive option. For PC users, it means right-clicking the top folder and selecting Send → ZIP.

When you have your ZIP file you can upload it to the PhoneGap Build site.

The Build servers will kick into high gear immediately and start converting your application. This process takes about five minutes depending on the size of the files you are uploading.

A very useful dashboard shows you where you are in the build process. A happy face icon lets you know that your HTML has been converted into an app. A sad face means something went wrong, as shown in Figure P5.4.

Nitobi is adding more functionality to the PhoneGap Build service that includes additional operating systems, and the ability to add custom icons and replace code.

Figure P5.4 The PhoneGap Build health chart.

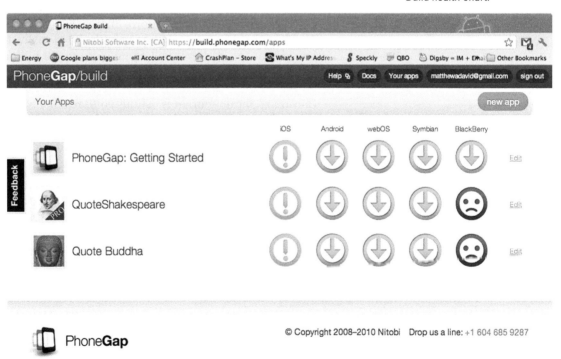

When the build process is done you will have links to all the apps in their native format. Here is the list:

- iOS apps are APP files
- Android apps are APK
- WebOS is IPD
- Symbian is WGZ
- BlackBerry is OTA

You will need the apps in their native format to submit to the many app stores.

Submitting to the App Stores

At one time it was easy to submit to an app store. There was only one: Apple's iTunes App Store. Then came Google's Android Market. And now there are over a dozen, from Intel's AppUp store to Amazon's Android App Store. Every Mobile OS has one or more app stores.

So which one do you target? The reality is that you need to target all of them.

The app marketplace is very much at the beginning of its lifecycle. There are currently approximately 600 million phones that are classified as smart phones being used globally. IDC has projected that this number will come close to 1.8 billion by the end of 2015. To put this into a frame of reference, the potential app market is 50% larger than the current PC/Mac market. By 2020 the smart phone market is estimated to reach 4 billion: Every two out of three people on the planet will have a smart phone.

This is a huge market!

Each market has its own requirements. You will also find that each market has a different process for reviewing apps. Google's Android Market will publish your app in less than two hours. The Amazon Android App Store will take as much as six weeks. You will need to work within the restrictions of each store. Try not to get too frustrated since all the stores are greatly improved over Apple's original delayed release schedule when the iTunes App Store first opened. My first app took two months to be published!

Making Money!

There are several reasons why you want to build an app: It may be to simply show your friends that you have built an app—this was my motivation when I got started—nothing like one-upping your smug, UNIX friends (wink).

Another reason may be more practical: You want to make money.

Mobile operating systems are providing more effective methods for making money with your applications. The three main techniques today are:

- Charge for the app
- In-app purchase
- Advertising

Charging for your app is a method of generating revenue. What I have found, however, is that you can increase the number of downloads you have for your app by running special sales. There are a large number of websites that track app sales. Start by selling your app at an introductory price; later, raise the price for two weeks and then drop it back down. You will see your sales jump.

The next method for increasing sales is through purchasing features from within your application.

A final, consistent tool for generating revenue is through advertising. Mobile advertising from companies such as Apple, Google, and Greystripe has matured dramatically. Today, it is widely believed that mobile ads are more effective than any other format of online advertising.

After you have defined which method you are going to use to monetize your app, your next step will be to market it. This includes asking for app reviews, starting a Twitter feed, and a hundred other activities. In many ways, you will put as much effort into marketing your app as you did publishing it.

Summary

In this project you have used a new mobile web framework, iUI. The framework is similar to jQuery Mobile and jQTouch. When you have finished with your HTML you can post the files to a website, or you can create a native application for sale in an app store.

The second part of the chapter placed a focus on converting your HTML into a native application for publication using Nitobi's PhoneGap Build cloud service. Through a few steps, you can convert a website into a native application.

The final step, once you have your application files, is to load the files to the different app stores and make some money.

In the next project, you will see how you can create solutions for tablets.

CREATING WEBSITES FOR iPAD AND ANDROID HONEYCOMB TABLETS

Got iPad? It is hard to imagine a time when there was not an iPad tablet. The low cost for purchasing the device, the ease of use, and the massive number of apps have altered our collective perception of what a tablet is.

Let's be clear: the tablet computer is not new. Microsoft developed the technology in 2000. Unfortunately, the Microsoft tablet was heavy, slow, and expensive.

In 2010 Apple released the iPad—a sleek, fast, and cost-effective product that is one of the most desired pieces of technology ever released. The world can't get enough of them.

Apple continues to dominate the tablet market with the release of iPad 2, shown in Figure 6.1. The desire for a tablet has not gone unnoticed. RIM has released the PlayBook, Google now has Honeycomb, a version of Android designed from the ground up for tablets, and HP is bringing its WebOS to a tablet near you. Sales of laptop computers are now dropping as customers choose tablets. A new communication tool has been released.

In this section we look into what you need to consider when developing for tablets. They are not simply big iPhones.

What Makes a Tablet a Unique User Experience?

Apple's release of the iPad in January 2010 involved an unusual presentation technique. A comfy chair sat in the center of the stage. Steve Jobs came on stage and sat down, looking like he was going to watch the Sunday football game. Instead he pulled out the iPad and changed the world.

Figure 6.1 The iPad 2.

The first reaction to the iPad was that it was an oversized iPhone. Who wants one of those?

But the iPad is not an oversized smart phone. Nor are any of the tablets on the market. A tablet in the current form factor is truly a new and unique technology experience. This is true of the Xoom, PlayBook, and all the competing tablets.

Smart phones are designed for instant content. You take out your Android phone, check the weather, your mail, and the news and put the phone away. Next time you are grocery shopping, watch as people casually check information on their phones as they are standing in line to pay.

The tablet, on the other hand, has an experience more akin to a book or magazine. You engage with a tablet. Your tablet is always on. Apps always use the whole screen, allowing you to focus just on the app and not be distracted by other content.

When Steve Jobs came on stage and sat in a comfy chair he was making a direct statement: your iPad allows you to fully engage with it.

The indirect statement Apple has made since is this: The days of the traditional computer are very much numbered.

There are an ever-increasing number of tablet computers entering the market. Today, and likely for the next couple of years, Apple's iPad will dominate. The growth of the tablet market has only just begun. You will soon see tablet sales in the hundreds of millions per year.

Now is the time to start assessing how you can make your website work on a tablet.

Elements of the Tablet Experience: Sidebars, Pop-overs, and Touch Interfaces

Today, Apple is driving the elements of the tablet user experience for a simple reason: the vast majority of tablets sold are iPads. For this reason, you are seeing Apple's UX teams drive the new user experience.

The first new feature is sidebars. A sidebar appears when a tablet is held in landscape mode as an area on the left-hand side of the screen. When the tablet is moved into a vertical position, the sidebar disappears and is replaced with a button that will open and close the sidebar.

The next feature is called a pop-over. Essentially, a pop-over is similar to a dialog window found on a desktop computer, as shown in Figure 6.2.

Some features, though new, extend the touch screen technique developed for the iPhone. You have pinch-to-zoom, tap, double-tap, and multi-touch gestures. Your customers will want to leverage these features as you build websites optimized for tablets.

The bottom line reality is that rapid adoption of tablets is blindsiding many people. For this reason, web technologies that support tablet interfaces are sketchy at best. Arguably, the most mature technology is Sencha's Touch framework.

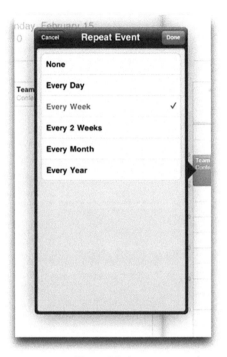

Figure 6.2 A pop-over on the iPad 2.

Using Sencha Touch for Tablet Creation

In earlier articles, you were introduced to Sencha Touch, a framework optimized for mobile devices. The initial list of devices includes iPhones, Androids, and BlackBerrys. Also on the list is support for the iPad.

The current support for iPad is somewhat limited. You have a sidebar that appears when the web page is viewed in landscape mode and disappears when resized to portrait.

The functionality to accomplish the sidebar using HTML is demonstrated in the default Kitchen Sink app that comes with Sencha Touch. You will need to download the Sencha Touch framework to view the Kitchen Sink sample.

The default file that controls the use of a tablet interface is labeled index.js and can be found in the SRC folder for the Kitchen Sink solution. Setting up the interface to work with the iPad takes more work than for the default iPhone. The challenge you have is detecting when the iPad is moved from vertical to horizontal, and whether the device viewing the page is an iPhone or an Android phone.

The first step is to create a new function that allows you to design for all user interfaces. In the following instance, the function is named UniversalUI.

```
Ext.ux.UniversalUI = Ext.extend(Ext.Panel, {
```

The following properties set the display to full screen with default presentation text:

```
fullscreen: true,
layout: 'card',
items: [{
cls: 'launchscreen',
html: '<div><img src="resources/img/sencha.png"
width="210" height="291" /><h1>Welcome to Sencha Touch</h1>
<p>This is a comprehensive collection of our examples in
an <br /> easy-to-navigate format. Each sample has a "view
source" button which dynamically displays its associated
code.<br /><br /><span>Sencha Touch (' + Ext.version +')
</span></p></div>'
}],
```

The following sets the left navigation menu to show if the screen is shown in landscape mode:

```
backText: 'Back',
useTitleAsBackText: true,
initComponent : function() {
    this.navigationButton = new Ext.Button({
        hidden: Ext.is.Phone || Ext.Viewport.
orientation == 'landscape',
        text: 'Navigation',
        handler: this.onNavButtonTap,
        scope: this
    });
    this.backButton = new Ext.Button({
        text: this.backText,
        ui: 'back',
        handler: this.onUiBack,
        hidden: true,
        scope: this
    });
    var btns = [this.navigationButton];
    if (Ext.is.Phone) {
        btns.unshift(this.backButton);
    }
    this.navigationBar = new Ext.Toolbar({
        ui: 'dark',
```

```
                    dock: 'top',
                    title: this.title,
                    items: btns.concat(this.buttons || [])
              });
```

The following functions are triggered by the iPad moving into portrait mode:

```
     this.navigationPanel = new Ext.NestedList({
          store: sink.StructureStore,
          useToolbar: Ext.is.Phone ? false : true,
          updateTitleText: false,
          dock: 'left',
          hidden: !Ext.is.Phone &&
Ext.Viewport.orientation == 'portrait',
          toolbar: Ext.is.Phone ? this.navigationBar : null,
          listeners: {
               itemtap: this.onNavPanelItemTap,
               scope: this
          }
     });
     this.navigationPanel.on('back', this.onNavBack,
this);
```

If the device is an iPhone or Android phone, the code will hide the left-hand navigation when the page is viewed in landscape mode. The width of the phone triggers if the sidebar is hidden when viewed in landscape mode:

```
     if (!Ext.is.Phone) {
          this.navigationPanel.setWidth(250);
     }
     this.dockedItems = this.dockedItems || [];
     this.dockedItems.unshift(this.navigationBar);
     if (!Ext.is.Phone && Ext.Viewport.orientation ==
'landscape') {
          this.dockedItems.unshift(this.navigationPanel);
     }
     else if (Ext.is.Phone) {
          this.items = this.items || [];
          this.items.unshift(this.navigationPanel);
     }
     this.addEvents('navigate');

     Ext.ux.UniversalUI.superclass.initComponent.call(this);
     },
```

The final result is that you can display new iPad-like features using Sencha Touch. The result, however, is clunky and requires a lot of JavaScript knowledge. There is no doubt in my mind that Sencha will improve tablet support over time but it is not quite there yet.

Using jQuery Mobile to Build Websites Optimized for Tablets

The most popular framework for quickly building smart phone websites is jQuery Mobile. At this time, jQuery Mobile does not support the iPad.

With that said, it does not mean you cannot create custom themes that give you iPad-like experiences. jQuery Mobile leverages CSS for visual presentation. All the position, border, padding, and other visual effect rules are controlled with the following CSS file you reference in the head of your page:

```
jquery.mobile-1.0a4.1.css
```

The CSS document can be opened in a text editor. There are two main sections to the CSS file:

- Defining the swatches to add colors, gradients, and text effects
- Defining the position of objects, rounded corners, and space

With a few keystrokes you can modify any of these elements to look and feel like elements found on an iPad. To this end, the jQuery Mobile team is looking at adding support for tablets in late 2011.

Building for the Future: CSS Regions

It is clear that support for tablets in web pages is limited at the moment. Fundamentally this is due not to widgets and features missing in frameworks, but to features in HTML that allow you to easily adapt your layout to different screens. A driving force at Adobe is multiscreen support; that is, you build one website that is optimized for desktop, laptop, iPhone, tablet, and interactive TV.

To address this problem, Adobe is proposing a new CSS property known as CSS Regions. Details surrounding CSS Regions can be found at *http://labs.adobe.com/technologies/cssregions/*.

The goal for CSS Regions is to allow you to develop one design that elegantly resizes, depending on the screen resolution, as shown in Figure 6.3.

The following example takes a simple approach of having some text wrap itself on three columns. There are two main elements to this example: CSS and HTML. No JavaScript was used in this demo (or hurt in any way).

Figure 6.3 A very early prototype of CSS Regions.

Start by declaring a standard HTML5 document:

```
<!DOCTYPE HTML>
<html>
<head>
      <title>CSS Regions - Simple Template Demo</title>
```

The CSS style begins with standard page presentation:

```
<style type="text/css">
body,
html{
      height:100%;
      width:100%;
      overflow:hidden;
}
body{
      margin:0;
      font-family: Helvetica, Arial, sans-serif;
      color:#222;
      font-size:15px;
      line-height:20px;
}
```

The source class is used to identify the block of HTML in the BODY element that will dynamically wrap content. To do this, a source class creates a –webkit-flow and names it main-thread.

```
#source{
     -webkit-flow: "main-thread";
     text-align:justify;
}
```

A CSS style named region inherits the main-thread as its source content.

```
.region{
     content:from(main-thread);
     margin:0 25px 0 0;
     background:#C5DFF0;
     padding:15px;
}
```

Three classes specify where on the screen the content will flow. You will see from the following settings that the size of each region is dynamically created depending on the size of the screen. This is demonstrating how content can flow from region to region.

```
#region1{
     width:20%;
     height:50%;
     float:left;
}

#region2{
     width:35%;
     height:170px;
     float:left;
}
#region3{
     width:20%;
     height:50%;
     margin-right:0;
}
#workspace{
     position:relative;
     padding:25px;
}
</style>
</head>
<body>
```

The following DIV element is the content that will be wrapped from one region to another. Here the content is just text, but you can add any type of HTML.

```
<div id="source">
    <p>Lorem ipsum dolor sit amet, consectetur adipiscing
elit. Fusce eros felis, eleifend at sagittis non, pulvinar
at ante. Maecenas cursus feugiat massa, sed ultrices mauris
mattis vel. Quisque volutpat hendrerit tristique. Quisque
a dolor sit amet metus convallis dignissim. Quisque id
volutpat orci. Lorem ipsum dolor sit amet, consectetur
adipiscing elit. Donec dictum augue id nisl mollis non
sagittis enim feugiat. Aliquam consectetur vehicula nibh et
euismod. Fusce posuere nisi eget enim auctor ut dignissim
neque gravida. Sed suscipit vehicula enim tempus tempus.
Aenean at felis id nibh lobortis auctor. Proin sodales
rutrum sollicitudin. Ut pharetra imperdiet sapien quis
venenatis. Quisque varius neque sem. Curabitur pharetra
condimentum ligula, quis imperdiet quam fringilla gravida.
Proin fringilla luctus leo ultricies molestie.</p>
    </div>
```

The following DIV element contains the three region areas where content will share the source content.

```
<div id="workspace">
    <div id="region1" class="region"></div>
    <div id="region2" class="region"></div>
    <div id="region3" class="region"></div>
</div>
</body>
</html>
```

When you view this page in a web browser that supports CSS Regions you will see that the content overflows into different regions depending on the size of the screen.

The specification is still very early in its development and will likely mature and change through 2011.

Summary

It is crystal clear that support for tablets is essential in your website design. What is less clear is the approach you take to support tablets. Frameworks, such as Sencha Touch and jQuery Mobile, are maturing to add support for tablets. In addition, Adobe is proposing core technology additions to CSS to add support for multiscreen devices.

The bottom line is that although these technologies are forward thinking, the future is rushing toward us. Forward-thinking solutions need to be implemented today for you to use. How we consume information on the web has changed forever: smart phones, tablets, interactive televisions, intelligent in-car systems, and so much more are driving this change. And your site needs to work on all of them.

PROJECT: DEVELOPING SOLUTIONS FOR TABLETS

Mobile development is not simply restricted to smart phones. There is a whole world of devices beyond phones. The popular category is now tablets, led by Apple's iPad but gaining solid competition from Google's Android Tablet OS, and BlackBerry's PlayBook. In Figure P6.1 you can see a picture of Apple's iPad. Tablets are following the innovative interface design popularized by the iPhone.

Building a website for a tablet is slightly different than building one for a smart phone. The size of the tablet, how you use it, and the processing power is different than a handheld phone. A tablet is really more like a computer than a smart phone.

With this in mind, you will want to design your website slightly differently for a tablet. In this project you will extend the current release of jQuery Mobile with a custom theme to illustrate how you can make a tablet experience different than a smart phone experience.

What You Will Need

To get started with this project you will need to download the files from *www.visualizetheweb.com*. The files for this project are contained in a ZIP file that you can extract on your desktop.

The project contains a lot of files. Many of the files are additional themes you can use.

Setting Up Your Project

The default project is a collection of calculators written in JavaScript that can be used on a tablet, as shown in Figure P6.2. The concept shows that you can use additional JavaScript libraries with jQuery Mobile.

Figure P6.1 Apple iPad tablet.

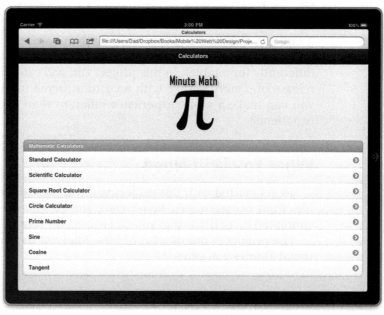

Figure P6.2 jQuery Mobile is being used to frame the app.

The core focus of the project is controlling the themes and structure of the elements. A second folder, labeled JQM-Themes, contains eight additional themes you can use on your site. To add the themes you only need to follow the next instructions.

The main document you will use is the index.html file. This loads the main theme and links to all the other files.

The HTML for the index.html looks like this:

```
<!DOCTYPE html>
<html>
<head>
<title>Calculator</title>
<link rel="stylesheet" href="jquery.mobile-1.0a2.css" />
<link rel="stylesheet" href="http://code.jquery.com/
mobile/1.0a4.1/jquery.mobile-1.0a4.1.min.css" />
    <script src="http://code.jquery.com/jquery-1.5.2.min.js">
</script>
    <script src="http://code.jquery.com/mobile/1.0a4.1/
jquery.mobile-1.0a4.1.min.js"></script>
    </head>
```

As you can see, the setup of the page is a standard jQuery Mobile HTML5 document. The rest of the page provides links to external web pages containing each calculator:

```
<body>
<div data-role="page" id="menu">
<div data-role="header">
<h1>Calculators</h1>
</div>
<div data-role="content">
<p align="center"> <img src="images/head.png"></P>
<ul data-role="listview" data-inset="true" data-
theme="c" data-dividertheme="b">
    <li data-role="list-divider">Mathematic Calculators</li>
    <li><a href="simple.html" rel="external">Standard
Calculator</a></li>
    <li><a href="scientific.html" rel="external">Scientific
Calculator</a></li>
    <li><a href="square.html" rel="external">Square Root
Calculator</a></li>
    <li><a href="circle.html" rel="external">Circle
Calculator</a></li>
    <li><a href="primeNumber.html" rel="external">Prime
Number</a></li>
    <li><a href="sine.html" rel="external">Sine</a></li>
    <li><a href="cosine.html" rel="external">Cosine</a></li>
    <li><a href="tangent.html" rel="external">Tangent</a>
</li>
    </ul>
    </div>
    </div>
    </body>
    </html>
```

Each link to a calculator uses the Rel attribute. This forces the link to release the Ajax session currently being used by jQuery Mobile.

Controlling Themes

Control over your graphical layout is essential as you design any website. You need to have colors blend with those of your company or client's brand. Buttons and tabs may need to be highlighted or muted.

On the whole, jQuery Mobile limits the use of image files to a minimum. Buttons, backgrounds, and tab bars are created using Cascading Style Sheets (CSS). There are some exceptions where you will use PNG images to control your layout, but this is the exception and not the rule. Page design with CSS has matured dramatically with CSS3 and has reached a point where you can use rounded corners and gradients to replace techniques that traditionally required JPEG or PNG images.

Most of your design can be controlled with CSS in jQuery Mobile. jQuery Mobile uses CSS to control the visual layout of content on the screen. There are two main sections for the CSS document:

- Structure
- Theme

The structure section of the CSS document controls the position, padding, and margins for elements such as buttons and tabs on the screen. The theme controls specific visual elements such as fonts, colors, gradients, shadows, and corners. Modifying a theme allows you to control the visual elements of objects such as buttons. An additional enhancement to a theme is the addition of a feature called swatches. A swatch sets the properties of a group of colors for a theme. Taking advantage of swatches allows you to easily switch in and out alternative color schemes from the main theme.

The default CSS document that comes with jQuery Mobile has a theme with a set of swatches right out of the bag.

You can switch out different color swatches for sections of your page. This is OK to start with, but what if you want to go further and control the visual layout of all the content you are looking at? Remember, you are using CSS to control all the visual content.

All the position, border, padding, and other visual effect rules are controlled with the following CSS file you reference in the head of your page: jquery.mobile-1.0a4.1.css.

You can open the CSS document in Dreamweaver or your favorite text editor. The style sheet consists of two main sections:

- Theme
- Structure

Themes control visual elements such as color, gradients, fonts, and shadows. Within the theme section of the CSS document is a section that controls how swatches are controlled.

The structure section of the document defines padding and placement of structural elements such as buttons.

Each of the pages in the project is controlled by jQuery Mobile themes.

Editing Swatches

Each of the swatches follows a similar structure. Each swatch is lead by a comment that identifies the swatch name. Five swatches (a, b, c, d, e) are included with the current release of jQuery Mobile.

Let's look at swatch a and examine how it formats the page. The first CSS class is:

```
/* A -------------------------------------------------
--------------------------------------------------------
----*/
.ui-bar-a {
  border: 1px solid #2A2A2A;
  background:#111111;
  color:#ffffff;
  font-weight: bold;
  text-shadow: 0 -1px 1px #000000;
  background-image: -moz-linear-gradient(top, #3c3c3c,
#111111);
  background-image: -webkit-gradient(linear,left
top,left bottom,color-stop(0,#3c3c3c),color-
stop(1,#111111));
  -ms-filter:
"progid:DXImageTransform.Microsoft.gradient(startColorStr=
'#3c3c3c', EndColorStr='#111111')"; }
```

The name of the class is special. It is labeled ui-bar-a. jQuery Mobile looks for the name of the suffix when the Data-theme attribute is added to an element. For instance, in the previous CSS example you need to define the Data-theme to be a. When this is selected the CSS class is used to format the toolbar in your page.

The final a is a variable that can be dynamically set. This allows for additional swatches to be easily created. For instance, you can change the swatch by using ui-bar-b.

The ui-bar class controls the footer and header toolbar. There are no images referenced. To create visual effects, the class relies on CSS3. You can use any of the text-shadow and gradient effects.

It is a good idea to start with small changes as you start to work your way through customizing the swatches in jQuery Mobile. For instance, in the following example, the only change is that the text color is now red instead of black:

```
.ui-bar-a {
  border: 1px solid #2A2A2A;
  background:#111111;
  color:red;
```

```
    font-weight: bold;
    text-shadow: 0 -1px 1px #000000;
    background-image: -moz-linear-gradient(top, #3c3c3c,
#111111);
    background-image: -webkit-gradient(linear,left
top,left bottom,color-stop(0,#3c3c3c),color-
stop(1,#111111));
      -ms-filter:
    "progid:DXImageTransform.Microsoft.gradient(startColorStr
='#3c3c3c', EndColorStr='#111111')"; }
```

Save the file and reload your page. You will see that the title in the header and footer is now red.

CSS offers you many different stylistic controls. Here you have made one change—the font is now red—but you can experiment with modifying the other properties. The one property that is challenging is the background-image property.

Background images take advantage of a new CSS3 property called gradients, used to fill in areas where the colors transform from one color to another. The earlier example has the gradient transforming from dark gray (3c3c3c) to white (111111) using the following properties:

```
    background-image: -moz-linear-gradient(top, #3c3c3c,
#111111);
    background-image: -webkit-gradient(linear,left
top,left bottom,color-stop(0,#3c3c3c),color-
stop(1,#111111));
      -ms-filter:
    "progid:DXImageTransform.Microsoft.gradient(startColorStr=
'#3c3c3c', EndColorStr='#111111')"; }
```

What is confusing is that there are three different ways in which a gradient is applied. The reason for this is due to different browsers supporting different ways of using a filter. In this example the first background image property is for Firefox web browsers, the second is for Apple's Safari and Google's Chrome, and the third setting supports Microsoft's Internet Explorer.

Each jQuery Mobile swatch has 26 different classes you can edit. You do not need to edit them all. In fact, you may want to copy the swatches and edit only the properties you want changed. The ZIP containing the documents used for this chapter has additional swatches. The approach used to modify each swatch was to copy the default a swatch and modify only the CSS properties needed. The rest is left the same.

Changing the Visual Elements

The first 600 lines of the CSS document (jquery.mobile-1.0a4.1.css) is dedicated to defining the five swatches that come with the default theme. The rest of the CSS document is used to

define general aspects of the theme such as the size of the roundness of the corners for the buttons. It is here that you can customize buttons for layout on a tablet screen.

The following example highlights the CSS classes for corner
roundness:

```
.ui-btn-corner-tl {
  -moz-border-radius-topleft: 1em;
  -webkit-border-top-left-radius:1em;
  border-top-left-radius:1em;
}
.ui-btn-corner-tr {
  -moz-border-radius-topright: 1em;
  -webkit-border-top-right-radius:1em;
  border-top-right-radius:1em;
}
.ui-btn-corner-bl {
  -moz-border-radius-bottomleft: 1em;
  -webkit-border-bottom-left-radius:1em;
  border-bottom-left-radius:1em;
}
.ui-btn-corner-br {
  -moz-border-radius-bottomright:1em;
  -webkit-border-bottom-right-radius: 1em;
  border-bottom-right-radius: 1em;
}
.ui-btn-corner-top {
  -moz-border-radius-topleft: 1em;
  -webkit-border-top-left-radius:1em;
  border-top-left-radius:1em;
  -moz-border-radius-topright: 1em;
  -webkit-border-top-right-radius:1em;
  border-top-right-radius:1em;
}
.ui-btn-corner-bottom {
  -moz-border-radius-bottomleft: 1em;
  -webkit-border-bottom-left-radius:1em;
  border-bottom-left-radius:1em;
  -moz-border-radius-bottomright:1em;
  -webkit-border-bottom-right-radius: 1em;
  border-bottom-right-radius: 1em;
}
.ui-btn-corner-right {
  -moz-border-radius-topright: 1em;
  -webkit-border-top-right-radius:1em;
  border-top-right-radius:1em;
  -moz-border-radius-bottomright:1em;
  -webkit-border-bottom-right-radius: 1em;
  border-bottom-right-radius: 1em;
}
.ui-btn-corner-left {
  -moz-border-radius-topleft: 1em;
```

```
    -webkit-border-top-left-radius:1em;
    border-top-left-radius:1em;
    -moz-border-radius-bottomleft: 1em;
    -webkit-border-bottom-left-radius:1em;
    border-bottom-left-radius:1em;
}
.ui-btn-corner-all {
    -moz-border-radius: 1em;
    -webkit-border-radius: 1em;
    border-radius: 1em;
}
```

Each of these classes is generic—they do not reference a specific swatch. The role of the swatch is to control color, font, and gradient effects. In the previous CSS classes, each class controls one element of a radius. Again, as we saw earlier, the inconsistent support of new CSS3 properties requires that each class have three properties that are essentially the same.

If you are going to create your own theme or modify the default theme then I recommend you make a copy of the default CSS document.

1. Open jquery.mobile-1.0a4.1.css in a text editor and save the file with a new name; for example: jquery.mobile.theme.css.
2. Change the roundness in the classes listed earlier (you will find them at line 601) to 0.1em.
3. Save your work.

In the HTML page, change the reference from the default jQuery Mobile CSS document to your new document. Save the page and preview on your tablet.

Coming Soon: ThemeRoller for jQuery Mobile

Controlling color with jQuery has been possible for some time with jQuery UI's ThemeRoller. A version of ThemeRoller that ships with jQuery UI is coming for jQuery Mobile. The jQuery Mobile ThemeRoller will be slightly different, but to get an idea of what is will likely look like you can preview the jQuery UI ThemeRoller at *http://jqueryui.com/themeroller/*.

Themes and swatches in jQuery Mobile, however, significantly improve on the efficiency of the original jQuery UI ThemeRoller. Gradients are controlled with CSS3 and not images. Indeed, CSS3 is used throughout jQuery Mobile to control rounded corners, text, drop shadows, and more.

Summary

Controlling the display of your website on a tablet can be driven with themes and swatches in jQuery Mobile. Moving forward, the jQuery Mobile team has already stated that it is

PROJECT: DEVELOPING SOLUTIONS FOR TABLETS **229**

working on a specialized version of ThemeRoller for jQuery Mobile. Although this will certainly make it easier to create themes for your mobile websites, it is important to understand why CSS are structured the way they are. Before you use ThemeRoller for jQuery Mobile I encourage you to write your CSS swatch file by hand. The jQuery team has done a great job to make this as easy as possible.

INDEX

Note: Page numbers followed by *b* indicate boxes, *f* indicate figures.

*For Product Safety Concerns and Information please contact
our EU representative GPSR@taylorandfrancis.com Taylor & Francis
Verlag GmbH, Kaufingerstraße 24, 80331 München, Germany*

T - #0170 - 090625 - C248 - 246/189/11 - PB - 9780240818139 - Gloss Lamination